DO IT ANYWAY

Do It Anyway

Anyway

The Next Generation of Activists

Courtney E. Martin

Beacon Press   Boston

Beacon Press
25 Beacon Street
Boston, Massachusetts 02108-2892
www.beacon.org

Beacon Press books
are published under the auspices of
the Unitarian Universalist Association of Congregations.

13 12 11 10 9 8 7 6 5 4 3 2 1

This book is printed on acid-free paper that meets the uncoated paper ANSI/
NISO specifications for permanence as revised in 1992.

Composition by Wilsted and Taylor Publishing Services

Library of Congress Cataloging-in-Publication Data

Martin, Courtney E.
  Do it anyway : the next generation of activists / Courtney E. Martin.
    p. cm.
  ISBN 978-0-8070-0047-2 (pbk. : alk. paper) 1. Social change—United States.
2. United States—Social conditions—21st century. I. Title.
  HM831.M3917 2010
  303.48'40922—dc22
  [B]   2010007766

For D. D.,
who taught me the necessity
of the examined life
and the tender heart

People are often unreasonable, irrational, and self-centered.
 Forgive them anyway.
If you are kind, people may accuse you of selfish, ulterior motives.
 Be kind anyway.
If you are successful, you will win some unfaithful friends and
 some genuine enemies. Succeed anyway.
If you are honest and sincere, people may deceive you.
 Be honest and sincere anyway.
What you spend years creating, others will destroy overnight.
 Create anyway.
If you find serenity and happiness, some may be jealous.
 Be happy anyway.
The good you do today will often be forgotten.
 Do good anyway.
Give the best you have and it will never be enough.
 Give your best anyway.
In the final analysis, it is between you and God.
It was never between you and them anyway.

—written on the wall in Mother Teresa's
home for children in Calcutta

Contents

Introduction

Save the world.

Where were you the first time you heard those three little words?

It's a phrase that has slipped off the tongues of hippie parents and well-intentioned teachers with a sort of cruel ease for the last three decades. In Evangelical churches and Jewish summer camps, on *3-2-1 Contact* and *Dora the Explorer*, even on MTV, we (America's youth) have been charged with the vaguest and most ethically dangerous of responsibilities: save the world. But what does it really mean? What has it ever really meant—when uttered by moms and ministers, by zany aunts and debate coaches—to save the whole wildly complex, horrifically hypocritical, overwhelmingly beautiful world?

I for one had no idea, but that didn't stop me from internalizing the message. I swallowed those three little words—a trio of radioactive seeds. They looked innocent enough when poured into my palm, but when swallowed, they buried themselves deep in my gut and started to grow. South African novelist J. M. Coetzee wrote, "All creatures come into the world bringing with them the memory of justice." Shortly thereafter, if all is right, the world breeds in us an outrage over injustice.

At first I engaged my outrage like a true-blue white girl from the suburbs. I sent letters to the managers of Arby's and Wendy's in my hometown, begging them to stop using Styrofoam cups in their establishments for the good of our Mother Earth. No response.

I volunteered in an assisted living facility, screaming the letter-number combinations for a comatose game of bingo. Though the residents attempted to adjust their hearing aids, my voice was too high to register. They screamed, "What? What did that girl say?" to one another, but everyone just shrugged and smiled at me sympathetically.

I worked at the local soup kitchen, dragging wet rags across Formica tables with my eyes diverted straight down, hoping none of the homeless people would actually speak to me. I was frightened by the ones that smelled, but even more frightened by the ones that didn't smell. The ones that looked like me and my mom. The ones that I'd seen walking around downtown and never even known I was supposed to save. I couldn't name it yet, but it was the first experience that called the conventional wisdom at the time—that there were savers and those to be saved, and that these were immutable categories—into question.

When Sally Struthers commercials came on, featuring little African babies with distended bellies and flies hovering around their eyes, I felt as if I had been punched in the stomach. I took it personally. After all, I had been charged with saving the world, as had my friends and little bike-riding neighbors. The adults in our lives had drawn a line directly between the suffering of the world—the African babies, the growing hole in the ozone layer, the homeless guy who lay listlessly on the bench outside the library—and our own nascent sense of purpose.

Once, agitated with one epiphany or another, I decided I would march around my neighborhood—middle class, suburban, white—and ask people for money for "the poor." I found an old glass jar in my playhouse, cleaned it fastidiously, and headed into the suburban wilderness for my first experience of fund-raising.

It went pretty well, actually. I was cute at the time—frizzy hair permanently set in a side ponytail, big blue-green eyes with dark, thick eyelashes, and a pair of magenta Converse high-tops (it was the eighties). I think that the smiling neighbors, pried from their daily dose of Oprah, took one look at me, heard my half-formed rationale, and sympathized with the familiar ache in my heart. They dropped quarters, sometimes even dollars, into my jar and sent me on my way.

I rounded the block, growing more and more excited about the efficiency of my tactic. By the time I returned to my play-house, I had over ten dollars. But as I sat on the wooden planks, my legs splayed, and pushed the coins around with my fingertips, a bad feeling started to creep over me. I realized that I had no idea who "the poor" really were.

I didn't know if I had met them before. There were kids at my school with less trendy clothes than all the others, but did this really mean they were poor or just that their parents were strict or stingy? There were those little babies with the bloated bellies on the commercial, but would ten dollars really help them? It seemed like they needed much more. I could find some of the homeless guys near the library, but they might spend the money on drugs (by age eight, I'd already heard this warning many times). And how would I choose which people to give the money to anyway? Who was the most deserving? How could you predict that they'd use it for good? What if you gave money to someone and they were insulted—angry that you assumed they needed it?

The questions washed over me like a tidal wave, and suddenly everything about my initial intention—so pure, so heartfelt— was murky. I piled the money back into the jar and stared at it disapprovingly. There is, perhaps, nothing more paralyzing than a good intention suddenly proven naive. I decided to bury the jar in the shadow of my playhouse until I knew what to do with it. If you go to 1718 North Tejon Street in Colorado Springs, you'll find that it's still buried there, along with my childhood illusions that "saving the world" is a simple or pure prospect.

SOCIAL SCIENTISTS AND THE MEDIA seem to have made an ugly habit in the last few years of labeling my generation (defined in this book as those thirty-five years old and under) as entitled, self-absorbed, and apathetic. Psychologist Jean M. Twenge, in *Generation Me: Why Today's Young Americans Are More Confident, Assertive, Entitled—and More Miserable Than Ever Before*, argues that, largely because of the boom in self-esteem education in the eighties and nineties, young people today "speak the language of the self as their native tongue." Tom Friedman dubbed us Generation Q, for quiet, in the pages of the *New York Times*, writing that "Generation Q may be too quiet, too online, for its own good, and for the country's own good." And morning shows can't resist a segment on how entitled Gen Yers are in the workplace and what their bosses can do to tame their positively gargantuan egos.

I think they've got it wrong. They're missing a class analysis. And they've mistaken symptoms for the disease. We are not, on the whole, entitled, self-absorbed, and apathetic. We're overwhelmed, empathic, and paralyzed. The privileged among us are told over and over that it is our charge to "save the world," but once in it, we realize that it's not so simple. The less privileged are gifted their own empty rhetoric: American Dream ideology that charges them with saving, perhaps not necessarily the whole damn world, but at the very least their families, their countries, their honor. We are the most educated, most wanted, most diverse generation in American history, and we are also the most conscious of complexity.

In *Let Your Life Speak*, Parker Palmer writes, "Absolutism and relativism have ravaged not only the things of the world but our sense of the knowing self as well. We are whiplashed between an arrogant overestimation of ourselves and a servile underestimation of ourselves, but the outcome is always the same: a distortion of the humble yet exalted reality of the human self, a paradoxical pearl of price." In other words, we know that—simply by virtue of being born at this time, in this place—we are privileged, and furthermore, responsible for sharing that privilege. But we also know that making good on either promise—saving the world or saving our families—is not nearly as simple as our kindergarten teachers or our aspirational parents made it sound.

We know that soup ladling isn't enough, that Western values are sometimes imposed on other cultures in the guise of good works, that charity often serves to disempower a person in the long run, that too many nonprofits are joyless and ineffective places, that we have so much to give and yet so little. We've watched our own parents—many of them immigrants with big American Dreams in bright lights—be disrespected by the supposed promised land. We've taken human rights and women's studies classes where first-world arrogance was put in sharp relief to third-world ingenuity. We've experienced the painful irony of walking our donation check, earmarked for Indonesian hurricane relief, to the mailbox in our own poor Oakland neighborhood, which we were gentrifying by our mere existence.

Perhaps most significantly, we experienced 9/11 right as we were developing a political consciousness. I was a senior in college, poised to enter the real world with a sort of indestructible bravado on September 10. On September 11, everything I'd understood about my own safety, about the implications of America's reputation throughout the world, about violence and poverty and extremism, was transformed. I became simultaneously more humble and also more committed to really examining the beauty and ugliness of the country I'd been so blessed to be born in. But that examination has not lead to any clear answers.

It's been worthwhile, but it's also been paralyzing. The war on terror may be an ill-conceived, inaccurate battle plan, but what do we do in the face of such hatred? Reinstating the draft would be a disaster, but how can we stand by as military recruiters prey on the most needy of young Americans? What is our individual responsibility to end war?

It's as if we each possess that glass jar, buried within, and it's growing heavier all the time, and we have no idea what the hell we're supposed to do with it.

WHEN I FIRST CONCEIVED of this book, it was out of very real desperation. I marched against the Iraq War, along with upwards of six million other people across the world, and President George Bush called it a "focus group." Despite all of my phone banking and wonky obsessing, he was reelected for a second term. The wars in Afghanistan and Iraq raged on. Abu Ghraib hit the headlines. The wealth disparity yawned larger and larger. My first nonprofit job was one long exercise in disillusion, and freelance writing was often alienating. I felt as if I had been sold a bill of goods. The world was a cruel, unjust place, and far from saving it, I felt stuck in it.

Looking for solace, I had lunch with my favorite professor from Barnard College, where I'd been an undergrad just a few years earlier. Professor Dalton was the one whose gospel of a true calling or *arete* (Plato), of a social contract (Rousseau), and of the power of love (King) had set me on fire at twenty years old. I would leave his class vibrating with grand notions of what it meant to live an ethical, examined life and how I might shape mine to reflect all this learning. Just five years later, I felt extinguished. The real world was not a place of perfect forms and pat answers. It was messy, bureaucratic, painful.

But instead of soothing me, my professor seemed to have his own desperation to battle. "Where is your generation's outrage?" he asked me. He told me stories of lecturing on the Holocaust, only to have one of his students ask, "Is this going to be on the test?" When I visited his classroom, slipping into a seat in the back, I saw laptop screens alight with Facebook and Zappos as he spoke passionately about the "miracle, mystery, and authority" of Dostoevsky.

The conspicuous lack of outrage, however, was not limited to the privileged. Consumerism and celebrity worship distracted the students that I worked with two afternoons a week at a low-income public high school. They were more interested in brand name bags and tight sneakers than fighting inequity. They wanted to know how they could get rich, not how the rich perpetuate systems of oppression.

And I couldn't really blame them. The political and cultural landscape circa 2005 prized status over courage, safety over innovation, and preprofessionalism over finding one's true calling. Anyone stubbornly dedicated to social change was destined for a harsh lesson in what Martin Seligman calls "learned helplessness": when one has grand expectations and finds them repeatedly unfulfilled, the unavoidable next stop is Despair. It was a time when the wind was knocked out of our collective sails. I was left standing on the shore of my own good intentions, wondering what ever happened to my dreams of "doing good."

AND THEN a new day dawned.

It would be hard to overstate Barack Obama's significance in terms of his influence on young people and our notions of good works. I'm not talking exclusively about the thousands upon thousands of young people who joined his campaign—knocking on doors, sending text messages, descending on Iowa and Florida. Of course, those kids were transformed forever by their experience of standing up with a leader they finally believed in.

But Obama's leadership has had a broader, even more profound effect on us. It's given us an opportunity to see our own sensibilities, our own idealism, our own complex identities reflected at the highest level. Barack Obama is the America we dreamed about when we were little kids sitting in that classroom with Doritos cheese under our fingernails. He is the grand symbol, the big victory, the fireworks that we so longed for.

Which is a blessing and a curse. On one hand, his election has made a lot of young people believe in the political process again, reflect on their own civic duty, and learn more about community organizing. On the other hand, all the hype that surrounded his candidacy has revived one of our more dangerous delusions—that "saving the world" is about heroics. In fact, the world will not be saved. It will be changed. It looks more like your mom—her palm on your fevered forehead, her handwritten schedule for sharing child care with neighbors, her letter to the editor of the local newspaper—than it does your president. Activism is a daily, even hourly, experiment in dedication, moral courage, and resilience.

THIS BOOK IS AN EXPLORATION of that effort. Initially I conceived of it as a way out of my own desperation. I wanted to meet young people who had figured out how to feel efficacious in a world that seems to do its damnedest to make us feel otherwise. Interestingly, I found that much of the most effective social change comes, initially, from a self-interested place and radiates from there. My own vulnerability was not a bad place to start.

I also wanted to create a book that served as an answer to my professor's query—"Where is your generation's outrage?" I wanted it to be a collection of profiles that proved the skeptics like Tom Friedman wrong. This is not a quiet generation; it is a generation searching for its own way. To older generations, that search is misinterpreted at best and invisible at worst—not because we aren't fighting, but because they don't recognize what the fight looks like anymore. It's rarely out in the streets. It's rarely dressed up in catchy slogans. But it's not all online either (a favorite misconception of boomer critics). It exists in defining moments—usually far from the glare of the television camera's eye or the flashing red light of the journalist's voice recorder. As I began to meet my subjects—to spend hours with them in their offices, riding in their cars, sharing meals—I began to see some of the larger implications of my journey through their lives. I was examining the minutiae of existence in a way that rightfully honors it. The media rarely do this. Instead we focus on the extraordinary, the luminous, the booming finale. I was more interested in the in-between—the confusion, the contradictions, the quiet seconds when a person wrestles with his or her own instincts.

Like anthropologist Mary Catherine Bateson, who wrote *Composing a Life,* about the daily choices contemporary women make, I wanted to excavate the often overlooked and hugely important little moments that make a person an activist. This is not a book analyzing best practices or systemic change; some of that discussion comes up organically in the context of these activists' daily struggles, but I claim to be no expert on social work, civic engagement, or community organizing. Instead, this is a book that takes a psychological lens to the very human pursuit of making a life that mends, at least in some small way, a broken world.

It's so often not the protest march or the foundation grant that defines us, but the far more personal stuff of life—being disappointed by mentors, being uplifted by the tiniest of interpersonal victories, pulling ourselves off the edge. It is twenty-six-year-old Dena Simmons teaching her eighth-grade class how to solve for x. It is thirty-five-year-old Raul Diaz listening to a young man's fears about leaving prison. It is twenty-six-year-old Tyrone Boucher walking out of his way to get a wrap at the farmers' market instead of grabbing lunch at a corporate chain.

The eight young people featured in this book are not superhuman. They haven't cured cancer or donated their kidneys to strangers or won millions of dollars in prize money. They are, instead, breathtakingly ordinary. They are courageous and flawed and visionary. They are smart and powerful and sometimes insecure. What sets them apart is that they have found an intersection where, as Frederick Buechner puts it, their "deep gladness and the world's deep hunger meet." Generally, they aren't satisfied. Or at least they are not any more satisfied than you and I. But they are satiated. Their work feeds them.

They are from a range of fields and geographical areas—a filmmaker in New York, a prison reentry social worker in East L.A., a radical philanthropist in Philly, an environmental justice advocate in D.C. They come from families where "save the world" was a charge by birth, and families where these words would never have been spoken, much less in English. Some of their activism was spurred by personal trauma—a sexual assault, neighborhood violence, illness—and some of it grew from a more privileged, more intellectual place—the recognition of injustice, the desire to contribute to the solution, bad old-fashioned guilt.

I found them through a truly organic process. I met them at schools, in conferences, through blogs. They were recommended to me by friends, old professors, even strangers. Once I became intrigued by their official biographies, I took time to learn a bit about their personal stories—convinced that both had to be compelling in order to build engaging narratives, and of course drawing on my own feminist wisdom that the personal is always political.

I was very intentional about getting young people who work in a range of fields, from a range of demographic backgrounds, but I was also cognizant of my limits. These are just eight people out of thousands the country over who are doing incredible work. There are large fields left out that I would have loved to explore— among them medicine, social entrepreneurship, and law. I also had limited funding to travel, so I regret that the majority of the activists profiled here are from the West or East Coast. I hope that other documentarians will pick up where I've left off.

A word on the domestic focus of the majority of those profiled: it is my strong belief that globalization and its effects demand that we, as Americans, get clear about the unmet needs and unanswered injustices in our own backyard. Not only do many of these enduring inequities—global warming, militarization, economic disparity—have global impacts, but our moral integrity depends on our capacity to deal with the suffering that surrounds us before we point the finger at others.

I admire so much of the work that young Americans are doing throughout the world, but I also fear that too many of us seek sainthood abroad; Rachel Corrie's profile illustrates the danger in this thinking, to some extent. Foreign problems can appear spuriously simple compared to those at home, which are so undeniably personal and seemingly intractable. I learned this when I studied abroad in Cape Town. I went eager to learn about the ways in which apartheid and its eventual defeat had affected the people there. Eventually I realized that part of my attraction to the place was that race relations seemed so black and white from an outsider's perspective, as opposed to the painful, gray shadows that made up my racialized American experience. I ended up learning far more about America than I did about South Africa in those six short months.

Thomas Merton wrote of an "invisible fecundity" and a "hidden wholeness" that exists within each of us. In these profiles, I aim to find the hidden wholeness in each of my subjects' lives. Writing about people inherently objectifies them. Though these profiles are substantial, they could never represent the true complexity of the human beings they describe. Instead, I've tried to present a collage of moments and ideas that honors each of them and teaches the rest of us something important. These are not PR profiles. Each of these activists is too thoughtful, too honest, to feel truly honored by a portrait that doesn't acknowledge their complexity, so you'll find that I examine them scars and all, challenge them, and at times compassionately critique the impact of their work.

You will also find a hidden wholeness, if you look closely, among the group at large. I was delighted by the ways in which these totally disparate human beings—none of them working directly together, most of them complete strangers—echoed each other across great distances and divides. They have sometimes traveled the same path, years apart. They have expressed parallel struggles, experienced the same places, asked the same questions. I'll revisit these larger trends and themes in the conclusion, but I encourage you to have fun spotting the moments when these perfect strangers appear exquisitely and unknowingly intertwined.

My gratitude toward them for allowing me to become part of their lives, and write it all down, is indescribable. It takes such confidence, such bravery, to allow a stranger—much less a journalist—inside. I would feel like a true cannibal unless I also knew that this process can be healing for people, that activists—especially—are so rarely honored with the sort of listening ear and finely tuned attention that I have tried to introduce with my presence.

Bucking journalistic conventions, I also involved each of them in my writing process—giving them a chance to read their profiles, give me feedback, and correct any inaccuracies. It's something that most traditional journalists wouldn't do, for fear that their subjects' involvement would get in the way of the Truth, but I think that objectivity is an ideal all but impossible for an engaged writer (and what other kind is there, really?). I suspect that a lot of traditional journalists don't show their work to their subjects before publication not because of a lofty commitment to so-called objectivity, but out of plain old fear. It's incredibly difficult to write about real people—especially if you aim to do it honestly—and then face their reactions. It scares the shit out of me every time, but it's critical to my own integrity. I think it's not only disingenuous to hide behind journalistic convention, but—especially in long form pieces like these—actually immoral.

I hope that each of my subjects feels truly, deeply seen in this experience. And I hope that you, the reader, see yourself in them. You don't have to be a celebrity to relate to Rosario Dawson's struggle for authenticity within her activism. You don't have to have been in the military to identify with Maricela Guzman's silence. You don't have to have grown up in the Bronx to understand Dena Simmons's love affair with home. Alasdair Macintyre wrote, "I can only answer the question 'What am I to do?' if I can answer the prior question 'Of what story or stories do I find myself a part?'" I hope you find yourself a part of these stories, as I have so profoundly.

This book is dedicated to abandoning the "save the world" and American Dream rhetoric for a language that is still inspiring, but also pragmatic—a language that we can use like a bridge over the chasm between what our parents and teachers told us about good deeds, about success, and what the real world needs every day. It is a call to transcend school-required community service and résumé-padding activities in favor of the kind of work that keeps you up at night because you believe in it so deeply. It is a warning against paralysis and the sort of numbing our generation has made ourselves infamous for (drinking, drugging, shopping). It is an invitation.

I invite you to read about these eight ordinary human beings' lives and believe that your life has the potential to be no less powerful. I invite you to see yourself in them, your silly dreams in their brave acts, your buried instincts for kindness and outrage in their insistence on change. Because, of course, they are no different from you and me—children of the eighties and nineties, inheritors of "save the world" anxiety, American dreamers, cynics, fragile and kind. They have just figured out a way to soothe the critics and pessimists in their own heads and act.

There are no real answers in this book, only insights and ca-tharsis. None of these activists knows the "right way" to create a more just world, nor do I. What we do know is that it's still worth-while to try. In these eight lives you will find thousands of noble attempts at healing the world's suffering, at making life more equitable and joyous for all. It is the smallness, not the largeness, of these attempts that make them worthy of examination.

Jane Addams once said, "We may either smother the divine fire of youth or we may feed it." I believe that outlandish expectations, crushing bureaucracies, out-of-touch political leaders, doomsday media coverage, and empty rhetoric about service and success only serve to suck the oxygen out of our hugely promising generation.

Instead we must look to one another for the spark. We must integrate lessons from the visionaries and pavement-pounders of yesteryear, but not become burned by waiting for their version of social change to manifest. Nor must we be relegated to sani-tized point-and-click activism alone. Technology aids us, but it doesn't define us. Our work, our hearts, our ingenuity are what determine our legacy.

TO BEGIN MY JOURNEY, I started at the end. A death. Perhaps I focused on the demise of a young activist first because it mirrored the dread that I harbored in my own soul at that time, the sense of desperation and despondency when it came to making real change in a world of so much suffering. I wanted to get up close to the biggest of sacrifices, to see how my own urgency and ano-mie could have played out were I not so in control, so tethered to my little world by family and friends who tried to protect me from my own sensitive nature.

For that, I would need to look at the life and death of Rachel Corrie.

"I Am Hungry for One Good Thing I Can Do"

Rachel Corrie, peace activist, Olympia, Washington

When Rachel got word that the Israeli bulldozers had revved up again, she would drop whatever she was doing, find her electric-orange jacket, grab her bullhorn, and head out to the site to serve as "bulldozer cowgirl," as she called it. She would stand directly between the giant yellow-orange metal machine and the small building in its path. Her body, thin and unassuming as it was, became the object of obstruction between the bulldozers and the homes, their gardens, the precious wells that surrounded their neighborhoods.

It's an interesting use of a body. It assumes that the body in front of the bulldozer is more valuable, more precious than the bodies inside the homes—even when there are six of them, mother, father, and children of assorted ages. Rachel's body was American, white, female. She grew up in Olympia, Washington, in a loving, liberal home. She wrote prolific diary entries and fantasized about being a humanitarian hero.

In 2002, at twenty-three years old, she ended up in Palestine and joined the International Solidarity Movement (ISM)—a motley crew of about six mostly young, mostly English-speaking international activists. One of the things they did on a regular basis was to face off against the Israeli army's forty-nine-ton Caterpillar bulldozers, driven by Israel's young sons and daughters who had been given orders to destroy homes thought to harbor terrorists. Not coincidentally, the Israeli army was also building a fourteen-meter-high wall along the border between Egypt and Gaza and needed to clear homes that were in the way.

Rachel wrote, "The surreal thing is that we are safe. White-skinned people stand up in front of the tanks and they open their weird tank lids and wave at us." Being arbitrarily born into a more valued, protected body was one of the privileges that Rachel bore with the most psychic turmoil. As a small girl she wrote, "In second grade there were classroom rules hanging from the ceiling. The only one I can remember now seems like it would be a good rule for life. 'Everyone must feel safe.' That's the best rule I can think of."

Many of Rachel's experiences with soldiers had a surreal quality of safety—smiles and waves in the foreground, guns and bulldozers in the background. She wrote, "Today as I walked on top of the rubble where homes once stood, Egyptian soldiers called to me from the other side of the border: 'Go! Go!' because a tank was coming. And then waving and 'What's your name?' Something disturbing about this friendly curiosity. It reminded me of how much, to some degree, we are all kids curious about other kids."

FROM AN ALARMINGLY YOUNG AGE, Rachel was curious about injustice in the world and had a vague notion that she must dedicate herself to ending it. At just nine years old, she wrote and read a poem for a school performance about ending global hunger. It glitters with naive audacity: "We have got to understand that the poor are all around us and we are ignoring them. . . . My dream is to stop hunger by the year 2000. . . . My dream is to save the 40,000 people who die each day."

A year later she penned an answer to that unavoidable inquiry of the ten-year-old state of mind—what will I be when I grow up? "I want to be a lawyer, a dancer, an actress, a mother, a wife, a children's author, a distance runner, a poet, a pianist, a pet store owner, an astronaut, an environmental and humanitarian activist, a psychiatrist, a ballet teacher, and the first woman president."

Call it nature—perhaps there was something about Rachel's innate personality or biochemistry or emotional alchemy that predisposed her to be sensitive and artistic and ambitious. Call it nurture—her parents were both deeply liberal, raising all three of their children to not only see suffering, but see themselves as responsible for its end, to value their own creativity. Rachel seemed inevitably pushed toward a life of angst and activism the same way some kids seem born to be pitchers or math wizards.

In those early years, Rachel wrote most about nature—"I must walk with care / as I wander in the wood / that I may crush no flower beneath my shoes"—and her relationships with friends and family—"People might think my mom is not a hero because she hasn't done anything 'exceptional.' Well . . . I know you *are* exceptional." Her world was small, fenced in by the Washington wilderness and the warmth of her family all around her.

But by thirteen, the world had grown less safe. Rachel started writing about death: "Death smells like homemade applesauce as it cooks on the stove. It is not the strangling sense of illness. It is not fear. It is freedom." At an age when most suburban teenagers are drunk on wine coolers and their own invincibility, Rachel seemed preternaturally aware of her own mortality. Her romance with death was adolescent, to be sure, but it was weighed down with the realization that death freed one from having to make decisions about what to do with a disproportionately valued body, how to use a privileged life.

A six-week summer trip to Russia satisfied all of her hunches about the unconsciousness of Americans. "I have never been so awake—so painfully, poignantly awake—as I was in Russia. The only thing my country told me when I returned was close your eyes. Go back to sleep again. I could not close my eyes to the incongruities of our nation."

It's not easy, of course, to live with eyes wide open in a world like ours. It ages people. That native audacity of Rachel's childhood performances was nearly extinguished by the time she returned from Russia, leaving in its place something like sober dedication: "I am hungry for one good thing I can do."

AS RACHEL WAS WRITING THESE WORDS in her journal on the bedroom floor of her little house in Olympia, Washington—perhaps lying on her belly, long feet kicking in the air as Pat Benatar (her favorite) blasted out of the stereo—the South Lebanon conflict was going into its tenth year a world away. An Israeli invasion of southern Lebanon in 1982 sparked ongoing fighting between the Lebanese National Resistance Front, including Hezbollah, and Israeli occupying forces, along with their ally, the South Lebanon Army. It would officially end in May 2000 when Israel forces withdrew and a tenuous peace resumed. On October 7, 2000, Hezbollah attacked Israel once again . . . and on . . . and on . . . and on.

Summarizing the Arab-Israeli conflict ethically is an impossible endeavor. It's a struggle so intractable, so emotional, so mired in nationalism and economics and religion and notions of home, that only the unaffiliated can see a faint outline of the big picture. And, of course, it is the deep emotional intensity that brings that picture into brutal focus, and that's something an outsider can't really see at all. The outline of the big picture is ultimately pretty worthless, as is the brutally focused image of just one tiny inch. It's a perfect representation of Gandhi's words, "An eye for an eye and the whole world goes blind." No one can actually *see* this conflict as a whole anymore.

Instead it gets cut up into little slices. A young woman, for example, raised in the middle of a beautiful wilderness in a family of do-gooder agnostics, easy to outrage and aching to do something significant with her life, something worldly, might hear about the ongoing violence in Israel and Palestine and latch on to the underdog. She might become incensed at the idea that a giant, well-funded, first-world military—one partially funded by her own bully of a country—is harming and displacing poor families. This young woman might latch on to the comfort of that one shining insight and let it lead her.

LIKE SO MANY TEENAGERS of her generation—the most wanted and coddled in history—Rachel had a nagging sense that she had been sold a bill of goods about her own specialness. At seventeen, writing about herself in the third person: "She had grown up believing that she had some special potential. She had had faith that there was a special purpose for her. Now that idea was cracking and shaking before her. She let the ache of disappointment carve into her and the doubt devour shredded bites of her soul."

Yet even while Rachel began to question her own destiny, she never fell into a state of helplessness. In fact, she found that although she could, at times, be uninspired to follow through on tasks to do with her own well-being—turning in a paper on time, getting enough sleep—she was endlessly inspired in her activism. She surprised even herself in her boundless energy to organize meetings and paint protest signs and study up on Afghanistan or Iraq.

In fact, she wrote down long lists of questions to follow up on in her journals. One right after the other they came: "How can I be of use? What does this peace movement need to look like? What resources do I need to analyze the local peace movements better? What are the historical parallels between this and past crises? What do I need to look at about myself?"

Rachel fell in love with a boy for the first time. Wrote pages and pages of abstract, smoldering poetry. Love ended.

She discovered cigarettes and drama, academic self-sabotage at Evergreen College, and a community of locals called the Olympia Movement for Justice and Peace. The over-the-hill hippies and young burnouts of OMJP became her people. They were hungry like her, or maybe just lonely enough to spend hours fashioning giant dove costumes out of papier-mâché and wire for the annual peace march—as long as it meant having the company of a firecracker like Rachel Corrie.

She worked at a mental health facility—first on the graveyard shift, then during the light of day—and consistently wrestled with categorization. "I have a rough time trying to articulate what I know about the work I do," she wrote. "We are all of us humans who need help, and we are all of us sometimes isolated by the things we perceive." While Rachel empathized deeply with the patients she encountered, she certainly didn't identify with them. One of the most surprising things about reading through all of the writings that Rachel left behind is the glaring absence of any indication that she herself was mentally unstable. Wildly imaginative and uncommonly passionate? Yes. But mentally unstable? Never.

Rachel had all this—the muse of lost love, the tight-knit community of activists, the "crazies" and their transcendent insights—but she was still unsatisfied, still hungering to be tested in an unavoidable way. Some part of her felt that she wasn't close enough to suffering—others' or her own. She wrote, "I have never known how to find a shell and then stay in it. I tend to wander out of the grotto when the sharks are attacking just to see what all the fuss is about."

A FEW YEARS BEFORE Rachel left home, she read Milan Kundera's *The Unbearable Lightness of Being,* a novel about love and sex and betrayal and fate, but mostly about the (im)possibility of life having real meaning. Kundera plays with Nietzsche's idea of "eternal return"—essentially that our lives and everything that happens within them are playing on an incessant loop with no end. That idea, Kundera posits, would make our actions, our experiences, our relationships inherently heavy with meaning, because we would know that they reoccur ad infinitum.

Instead, he argues, it is more likely that our lives play out along one finite line—that they end, not to begin again, and therefore are tragically light with meaning. And this is unbearable, because we ache to matter, to be of some import, and instead are doomed to be blips on a horizontal line of humanity.

Rachel devoured the book in one sitting and then reflected in her journal:

> The Lightness. Between life and death there are no dimensions at all. There are no rules or mile markers. It's just a shrug. The difference between Hitler and my mother, the difference between Whitney Houston and a Russian mother watching her son fall through the sidewalk and boil to death. There are no rules. There is no fairness. There are no guarantees. No warrantees on anything. It's all just a shrug. The difference between ecstasy and misery is just a shrug. And with that enormous shrug there, the shrug between me being and me not being—how could I be a poet? How could I believe in a truth? And I knew, back then, that the shrug would happen at the end of my life. I knew. And I thought, so who cares? If my whole life is going to amount to one shrug and a shake of the head, who cares if it comes in eighty years or at 8 p.m.? Who cares?
>
> Now. I know who cares. I know if I die at 11:15 p.m. or at ninety-seven years. I know. And I know it's me. That's my job.

7

Rachel, like so many of us, encompassed paradox. On the one hand, she recognized her own lightness. She was truly humble and sometimes even a tad cynical in much of her writings:

> This rant is the result of the sinking realization that the best of what we do is mitigation.
> I can't cool boiling waters in Russia. I can't be Picasso. I can't be Jesus. I can't save the planet single-handedly. I can wash dishes.
> Thinking it over, I realized that the most powerful action I can take toward societal improvement will have to start very close to home, arising not from the need to leave a mark on history, but from empathy and sincere understanding of the place in my life where neglect exists.

But there was also a part of her, it seems, that was unusually hungry for a heaviness, that was uncommonly convinced of her own importance—not in the sense of specialness, but in the sense of responsibility. It was the part of her that wouldn't, couldn't wait, stay home, and truly explore the issues in her own backyard. It was that part that got her listening so intently when she met some young world-wanderers who had been part of the International Solidarity Movement in Palestine and told her about the work that needed to be done there. It was that part of her that wrote "I need to go," that reordered her passport and got immunizations and traveler's checks and wrote down a list of people in the United States who might help her in case of arrest. It was that part of her that said good-bye to her mother and got on the plane and talked her way through customs in Israel.

It was that part of her that dreamed over and over again of her own demise: "Had a dream about falling, falling to my death off of something dusty and smooth and crumbling like the cliffs in Utah."

———

RACHEL WAS THERE for only three months before she was killed, in much the same way as she had dreamed it. While trying to prevent a Palestinian home in the Gaza Strip from being destroyed, on March 16, 2003, she was crushed by an Israeli bulldozer. One could argue that the moment when her slender body was sucked under a cloud of rubble and forty-nine tons of machine, as her whole being was subsumed by dust, her lungs crushed, her skull broken—*that* was the moment when her life became undeniably heavy.

Pictures of Rachel in her electric-orange construction jacket, holding her megaphone high, her feet firmly planted on the red earth, were published all over the world just hours after she was declared dead. Eloquent e-mails that she had sent her mother, Cindy, and father, Craig, were published in the U.K. *Guardian*. Palestinians immediately declared her a martyr, put up posters of her pale face above the word "peacemaker" throughout Gaza's streets, and held an emotional memorial for her. Some Israelis defamed her, immediately making the case that she'd been manipulated by terrorists into an untimely death.

A foundation was established in her name. The Corries filed lawsuits against the State of Israel, the Israel Defense Forces, and Caterpillar—the manufacturer of the bulldozer that crushed their daughter.

A book of Rachel's writings was published by W. W. Norton. A play was created from her diaries and letters—prompting heated debate in London, New York, and elsewhere, inspiring prizewinning playwrights like Tony Kushner and Harold Pinter to come to her defense, creating a conversation about the meaning of art and its role in politics.

Web sites deriding Rachel and the ISM popped up; others appeared in her defense, filled with links to eyewitness accounts of her death, human rights reports, chilling photographs of blood pouring from Rachel's face, her legs folded under her body like a newborn lamb. *Mother Jones* magazine did a somewhat damning investigative report on her death, claiming that in fact, the bulldozer driver couldn't see Rachel and that the ISM was known for its loose cannons, its young-and-dumb peaceniks, that it wasn't even embraced by many Palestinians. Cindy Corrie published her side in the *Boston Globe*. And on . . . and on . . . and on.

Five years later, it is as if Rachel has been destroyed twice. Once by an Israeli soldier who may or may not have been able to see her that day. And once by the crush of controversy that followed her death, the paper and the sounds and the fury essentially burying the humanity of this young woman who—above all else—wanted to stop suffering.

The notion that Rachel was somehow brainwashed by Palestinian radicals into putting her body on the line is not only patronizing and perhaps a little sexist, but incongruent with the woman found in all these beautiful words. While in Palestine, Rachel *did* learn more about the political complexities of the Arab-Israeli conflict. She wrote e-mails to her parents trying to explain why Palestinian violence was not justified, but surely was understandable. She was committed to keeping the Israeli military and actions of the state separate from the Israeli people in her impressionable mind: "I absolutely abhor the use of polarities like 'good' and 'evil'—especially when applied to human beings. I think these words are the enemy of critical thinking."

Far from being enraptured by some sort of terrorist-inspired death wish, Rachel spent her last days focused on the future. In an e-mail to her father on March 12, 2003, the day before she died, she wrote, "Don't worry about me too much, right now I am most concerned that we are not being effective. I still don't feel particularly at risk. . . . Let me know if you have any ideas about what I should do with the rest of my life."

If Rachel was seized by any rapturous allegiance around this time, it was only the humble beauty and perseverance of Palestinian families. She described an evening with one such family to her mom: "The two front rooms of their home are unusable because gunshots have been fired through the walls, so the whole family—three kids and two parents—sleep in the parents' bedroom. I sleep next to the youngest daughter, Iman, and we all share blankets." It is that kind of intimacy, surely, not the propaganda of anti-Semites, that moved Rachel to stand unmoving in front of that bulldozer that day. She wrote of the family she had come to know: "I am amazed at their strength in being able to defend such a large degree of their humanity—laughter, generosity, family time—against the incredible horror occurring in their lives and against the constant presence of death."

For Rachel, standing between a massive military machine and a humble family home was not a political act per se. It also wasn't messianic. It was what was right in front of her. It was the suffering that intersected with her own privileged life right at the moment when she was looking for meaning. It was a chance to stave off the "constant presence of death" for one more day for a family whose members had opened their home and shared their blankets with her. It was both the unbearable lightness and the profound heaviness of being. It was washing dishes.

JANET MALCOLM ONCE WROTE, "We choose the dead because of our tie to them, our identification with them. Their helplessness, passivity, vulnerability is our own. We all yearn toward the state of inanition, the condition of harmlessness, where we are perforce lovable and fragile. It is only by a great effort that we rouse ourselves to act, to fight, to struggle to be heard above the wind, to crush flowers as we walk. To behave like *live people*."

Reading about Rachel's life and death, spending time with her own words, imagining the deeper explanations behind some of her actions, I am reminded of how irresistible and yet how deeply false the romance of young death really is. For Rachel's mother and father, for her siblings, for her friends, she is no more. For the world, in fact, she is no more.

Living is hard as hell. True. Making daily choices about how to use our lives, how to leave our little corners of the world better than we found them, how to eat and speak and love ethically—it's enough to make one jealous of the seeming simplicity of Rachel's "one good thing." But we must resist that urge. Rachel is dead, and so are all of her possibilities. We must not envy that end, but turn to "live people" for our inspiration—the kind that still search, listen, show up, scream, and yes, "crush flowers as we walk."

An Altar Boy with a Gun

Raul Diaz, prison reentry social worker, Los Angeles

Raul Diaz is crushing flowers underfoot as he runs. Though he doesn't have the stamina of his teenage years of cross-country and baseball, he's grateful that his legs can still take him up a hill at thirty-four. He needs that perspective. He pauses at the top of a slope in Elysian Park, puts his hands on his hips, and looks out—his deep brown eyes surveying Los Angeles, the city that has formed him in all of its beauty and violence. Giant palm trees frame the scene—anxious traffic winds between houses painted in cheery pastels, and beyond, tall gray buildings stand innocuous, their edges blurred by the distance and smog. He can almost make out the outlines of Boyle Heights, his courageous little neighborhood—just east of downtown L.A. and the Los Angeles River, César E. Chávez Avenue rolling boldly through.

Up here, surrounded by deep green, his breath crackling in his chest, Raul can get a break from life down there—the way the boys drag their feet as they head back to their cells in Chino when his visits with them are over, the sadly predictable swollen bellies on teenage girls hanging out in the project playground in the unforgiving afternoon heat, the incessant needs of his clients (housing, jobs, work clothes, car insurance, food), unmet unless he figures out a way to meet them.

He runs up here because it's a way to leave all that behind.

13

But even more, he runs up here because he has never figured out any other way of staving off the sadness. As Morgan Freeman's character, Red, says in a movie that stuck in Raul's mind, *The Shawshank Redemption,* "Hope is a dangerous thing. Hope can drive a man insane."

THE YOUNGEST OF EIGHT BROTHERS, Raul was raised by one firecracker mom, Guadalupe (Lupe to her friends) Loera, who can cook up a chorizo storm and isn't afraid to take to the streets in search of one of her sons. She fled an abusive husband, the father of her six initial sons, in Texas (her family's home since crossing the border from Mexico in 1892). She relocated to the Pico projects of Boyle Heights without a single friend in 1968. ("All roads lead to Boyle Heights" is a frequent saying, reflecting the long history of the neighborhood as a first stop for arriving immigrants.) Guadalupe got a job at a print shop, a place where she would work for minimum wage for fifteen years without complaint.

In the early seventies, she met Raul's father—a Vietnam vet—who would end up shirking responsibility for his two kids. By the time Raul was five years old, his father was mostly absent, with the exception of a few random Saturdays when he would pull into the parking lot of the projects and start drinking. On those days he might show one of the boys how to fix a car or give them advice about girls, but Raul mostly stayed away.

"Why was that?" I ask, trying to picture Raul as a young, undoubtedly chubby-cheeked kid, resisting the impulse to run out and greet his dad.

"Don't get me wrong, Courtney," he says. "I wanted a dad, but I also watched the way these two neighbor kids responded every time their dad visited for the weekend. They wanted nothing to do with him. At first I was confused, but then I realized that not having a dad at all was sometimes better than having one that abused you."

Plus, Raul had Father Greg Boyle.

On Halloween night 1985, one of Raul's brothers was shot and ended up in the emergency room. Guadalupe sat rocking and praying in the waiting room of County General Hospital, tiny Raul by her side, wishing he were older and could somehow make it all right. A lanky white priest with a beard appeared, as if out of nowhere, and gave Guadalupe a huge hug. They'd never met before, but he calmly assured her, "Everything will be okay."

HOMEBOY INDUSTRIES, a center for at-risk and formerly gang-involved youth to get job placement, training, and education, is a modern, orange building—large and shiny among the land-scape of parking lots filled with school buses, beauty supply warehouses, and an elevated train that slinks into a station right on the edge of Chinatown. Inside, the waiting room is packed. Mostly guys, but a few young women, fill the twenty-five seats in the lobby, and about a dozen more mill about watching CNN on a large flat-screen television. Two security guards with earpieces stand next to the check-in desk and survey the crowd, looking for rival gang members eyeing one another up. A few younger guys sit behind the desk, making sure that everyone who enters signs in, including me.

"Who you here for?" a guy with a prominent tattoo on his neck and a great smile asks.

"Raul Diaz," I answer.

"Oh, Rulies? He's upstairs, probably. Just sign in and you can go up." His community has called him "Rulies" for so long that Raul has forgotten how he got the nickname in the first place.

Indeed, I find Raul in the upstairs hallway, talking to some kids in blue and khaki vests (the uniform for Homeboy employ-ees in training). He's wearing a black button-up shirt, dark jeans, and black leather shoes; he prides himself on looking nice—"business casual"—and setting an example for the boys.

Raul gives me a warm hug, even though we met for the first time only the day before, and we start the tour. Homeboy Industries resembles any modern office environment—cubicles in the center, small offices lining the outside, a groaning copy machine, lots of metal file cabinets, even a lounge where a plate of cookies has been left for staff members. Raul introduces me to the head of development, who has a grandmotherly fierceness about her. She gives me some press clips (*Wall Street Journal, Los Angeles Times, Newsweek*) and an invitation to the upcoming fund-raising dinner—hosted by *Lost* cocreator J. J. Abrams.

Homeboy Industries has come a long way since its origins in the Lord Mission Church twenty-plus years ago. Father Greg Boyle, now a celebrity of sorts, was just an unusually committed and daring Catholic priest back then, determined to show the gangbangers of Boyle Heights that there was more to life than turf wars and drugs. He tried to entice young guys like Raul into the church through youth groups and work opportunities. He also helped catalyze "the neighborhood ladies," as Raul affectionately calls them, to form a parents' organization called Comite por Paz en el Barrio (the Committee for Peace in the Barrio). Raul's own mother, Guadalupe, was the president.

Recognizing that many of the sons and daughters of Boyle Heights fell into gangbanging because there were no viable alternatives, Father Boyle and the ladies started approaching local businesses to see if they would hire the kids—attesting to their innate goodness and lack of opportunities. Their grassroots effort evolved into Homeboy Industries' current incarnation.

Today, Homeboy Industries is funded mostly by private donors and serves twelve thousand people a year—eight thousand gang members and four thousand gang-impacted youth between eighteen and twenty-five. (These figures don't include the countless people who are helped outside the building in countless little ways.) It provides young men and women with training in several types of jobs: baking, catering, and service through the Homegirl Café; retail and silk screening through the on-site store, which features T-shirts, coffee mugs, onesies, and Celeste Fremon's exhaustively researched book about Father Greg Boyle, *G-Dog and the Homeboys*; landscaping; clerical work (including basic computer skills); and most recently, solar panel creation and installation. The youngest employees also take classes during the day in everything from parenting skills to meditation. Most of those who come through the building have a gang tattoo or two removed in the clinic on the first floor, staffed entirely by volunteer doctors.

Raul has been part of this world, in one form or another, since he was a child, so walking through the halls with him is punctuated by frequent pounds and hugs. The enticing smell of freshly baked bread wafts up from the first-floor bakery. Everything is shiny and new—no tagging, no sagging. All the young people that mill about are in Homebody Industry T-shirts and clean, pressed pants. They aren't allowed to listen to their iPods or talk on their cell phones, so instead they shoot the shit with one another. There is a constant buzz of flirtation and inside jokes.

As we curve around past the classrooms—filled with young people—and along a hallway lined with photo collages of clients past and current, we run into Alex. He's about five foot four and wears black-framed dark glasses, his head shaved, his Homeboy Industries T-shirt oversized. "Tell her your story, Alex. She's a writer," Raul instructs.

Alex launches in, starting with how many bullets are lodged in his body (seven) and insisting that I feel the one that is just under the surface of the skin on his neck—an immediate intimacy that startles me. He's been blind for fourteen years, but still gangbanged for ten of them. "My homies would just put a gun and a bag of drugs in my lap and I'd be good," he says. About halfway through his spoken-word poem—a cross between gangster rap bravado and born-again inspiration—I realize that Alex is used to performing his story for visiting journalists and donors on cue. I feel a little gross, like the ex-gangster is tap dancing for his supper and I'm the one who is supposed to provide it. That feeling is confirmed when he says, "I've got cards downstairs if you want to drop by on your way out."

Later, when I ask Raul about this—the danger of being so identified with one particular way of telling your story, and the lure of shocking white folks like me with it to get attention and money—he nods his head knowingly. "Courtney, to be honest, I've thought about that a lot. That's why I was wary when Duncan first told me about your project, but I trust him and I said, 'Is she good people?' He said 'Yes,' and that's all I needed to hear." (Duncan is the mutual friend who introduced us.)

It's a quintessential response from Raul, whose worldview has been so largely shaped by the importance of loyalty. In Boyle Heights, you are either with us or against us, down or out, a homie or a rival. The genius of Raul is that he has always managed to escape these black-and-white definitions. Through his spot-on intuition and his subtle creativity, he has lived in many worlds—the gangster's, the athlete's, the prisoner's, the educator's, the community organizer's, the priest's—and yet belonged to none of them. All at the same time.

This is not to say that Raul is without ego. He appears to have a sort of attraction to the dramatic and sees himself as uniquely equipped to be at the center of it. I don't know whether it's a natural result of living in a neighborhood filled with Shakespearean rivalries, tragedies, and death, or if it's a personality trait, but Raul seems almost perversely comfortable in the middle of absolute devastation.

BASEBALL WAS LIKE A RELIGION in Raul's family. All the brothers played, and when they weren't hitting or playing catch, they were running around Elysian Park near Dodger Stadium. "While everyone else was selling dope," Raul says, "I was running. Other guys in the neighborhood would see my brothers and I and make fun of us—'Those fools are always running.' But I liked that kind of recognition."

It was an especially important distraction in the early nineties. Raul remembers that the summer of '92, when he was fifteen, was "extremely ugly—high-power assault rifles on every corner, gang violence out of control, crack everywhere." Indeed, in 1992 there were 2,113 homicides (803 of them gang-related) in Los Angeles, the highest in its history. Pico Gardens and Aliso Village, where Raul lived, combined to form the largest housing project west of the Mississippi. According to Celeste Fremon, within the square mile that made up the project's boundaries, seven Latino gangs and one African American gang warred— sometimes claiming as little as one solid block as turf valuable enough to be defended to the death.

Raul went to Roosevelt High School, where 82 percent of students are currently on free or reduced lunch and the graduation rate hovers around 50 percent. He knew he wanted to graduate, in part because he'd once been given a Brown University college sweatshirt (he can't remember by whom). He wore it all the time. Friends would ask, "What's Brown?" And he would answer, "A university in New York or some shit. I don't know." He loved tracing his finger over the letters and imagining what a college filled with Mexicans ("brown") would be like.

In truth, Raul didn't even learn how to read until eleventh grade, when a particularly enthusiastic English teacher named Ms. Wells got the kids to perform *Othello* in class. "I started digging it real fast," he says. The themes of jealousy, revenge, and allegiances—forged and broken—seemed all too relevant. Until that point he'd been shuffled between English as a second language classes, though English was always his first language, and special education. His intelligence was obviously underestimated.

What's so evident from Raul's stories of growing up in Boyle Heights is that it was his mother (isn't it always?) and his emotional intelligence—the capacity to identify and honor his emotions—that saved him. At sixteen, as a rare counterexample, he remembers convincing his mom to let him go to a party. It was the era of Dr. Dre and Snoop Dogg, and Raul had just tried gin and juice for the first time. He had a feeling in the pit of his stomach that he shouldn't go: "We were on our way there. I was in the back seat of the car, and suddenly I realize that I'm in a drive-by. One of the guys in the front seat pulls out a gun and just starts shooting. I was in shock.

"I never spoke about it again, but I decided right there that I would walk away from anything that didn't feel right the second it hit me," he says.

Raul was incredibly lucky. According to Fremon, a teenager at a similar time in a similar circumstance (no prior convictions, no weapon on him) was sentenced to thirty-five years to life in a Level 4 (the highest security level) adult prison as part of the crackdown on gang violence that swept the nation in the early nineties. Misguided criminologists talked about the new "superpredators" haunting the nation's streets, filling average Americans with fear and motivating politicians to campaign on tough-on-crime rhetoric that actually did nothing to prevent or treat the epidemic of violence among urban youth.

Some of Raul's older brothers were getting involved in drugs and violence, and he saw the way it tortured his mom. He knew she didn't need one more wayward son. Raul went to Wednesday night confirmation classes, where Father Boyle taught him to "love your neighbor and your enemies." He didn't go to Sunday Mass as often, but when he did, he remembers it feeling really good to talk to someone. He would say to God, "Hey, my heart hurts. My heart *and* my brain hurt. Help me get through this."

Raul's brain hurt because, in part, he was so busy navigating the double binds of his young life. Be tough, but not too tough or you might get challenged. Be cool with the hard-core guys, but not too cool or you might get jumped in the gang. Be aware, but not too aware or you might get caught up. "Caught up" is a perfect way to describe the lure of gang life in Boyle Heights. It just sort of happens. For young people with little parental presence, the family support of a gang can feel like a no-brainer. Especially when gangs are so rampant; according to Fremon, there were sixty different gangs in the sixteen square miles of Boyle Heights when Raul was coming of age.

He believes that it was his instincts that kept him from letting the tide take him along. "I sort of felt like an insider looking at the outsiders looking at me, if that makes any sense," he explains. "I knew all the street politics, but I wasn't involved, really. My guts kept me away. I had one foot in, but the rest of my body was out. Let's put it this way, Courtney: I was an altar boy with a gun."

RAUL SAYS HE WANTS to take me to lunch for some "real Mexican food." We sit across from one another in a booth sipping on giant drinks—Coke for him, horchata for me—and talk about his clients. There's something about the blaring Spanish music in this Mexican mall, the chaos of all of the vendors selling cheap toys and cowboy boots and knock-off bags that make it feel safe to speak on such difficult subjects. The chaos surrounds us like insulation.

"The guys have three minutes to eat sometimes, five minutes to shower. They're not treated like human beings," Raul says, the anger visible on his face. He and two other case managers at Homeboy Industries are currently nearing the end of a two-year grant from the Department of Juvenile Justice, the purpose of which is to help young people from the L.A. County area between the ages of eighteen and twenty-five reenter the real world after incarceration. Raul's caseload of sixty is filled with "hard-core" guys—murderers and drug offenders; the public defender's office started referring the most difficult cases his way after realizing how successful he was at cracking their previously impenetrable facades.

Raul's job description is technically "case manager," but "rehumanizer" sounds more appropriate. What he does with his clients goes far deeper than preparing their "reentry plans"—housing, job training, mental health services, and so on. He meets with them frequently, gets to know them through a series of intuitive questions about the relationships they've had—*Where's your dad at?* Usually in prison or missing. *Where's your mom at?* If no mom—*How was foster care? How was your social worker?* Raul will talk with them about baseball, the never-ending drama with the corrections officers (most of whom don't like Raul because he tries to circumvent the prison bureaucracies), their families back in Boyle Heights, even their crimes.

Raul is all instincts. He describes an exercise that he made up and uses frequently with clients to get them to reflect on their crimes: "I pretend to be the victim: I kissed my daughter this morning. Hugged my wife before I left the house. Headed out to get a loaf of bread and some milk, and your punk ass came to the bus stop and robbed me at four a.m. Do you know what it was like to have a gun in my face? When you robbed me, you robbed my pride, you took away my balls."

At this point, some of his clients will still act hard about it, at which point Raul breaks out the mom card: "How would you feel if it was your mom standing at that bus stop at four a.m. and some hard-core guy came and put a gun in her face? You rob people of their freedom when you do this shit, dog. You make them feel like they can't be safe in their own community. So you tell me, should you get parole yet?"

Many of them will simply say no, their eyes softened by the mention of their mothers, the "gangster mentality," as Raul refers to it, cracked. Some say yes: *The ultimate punishment is to parole me. I got nobody.*

"That's where the relationship really starts," Raul reports. "That's when I really gain their trust, because they know that I see the truth about what they've done and I'm still going to care about them."

Thirty to ninety days prior to a client's release date, Raul starts asking different kinds of questions—*Are you ready to get out?* Surprisingly, many aren't. They often feel as if they have no anchor on the outside. Some literally have no home until Raul figures out a place for them to stay. *What is your biggest fear about being back?* Number one: getting killed. Number two: having sex for the first time. Raul says, "They'll admit it to me: 'I'm scared to be with a woman, dog.'"

Add sexual educator to Raul's list of roles; he's explained the basics of intercourse and contraception more times than he'd like to remember. Many of his clients, after all, have been incarcerated in one form or another since they were twelve years old. Sex has taken on a pernicious presence in many of their lives from a young age. If they are caught masturbating in prison—and many are—they are charged with "sexual harassment" and three months are added to their sentences. Many of them talk about "those fools playing sex games"—referring to the homosexual sex that goes on within the prison walls—but none have admitted to being involved. Raul estimates that at least a quarter of his current caseload have been sexually abused in the past. When I ask about physical abuse, he scoffs and then says, "One hundred percent, no question."

"If you could change just one thing about the system, what would it be?" I ask, overwhelmed by how completely broken the whole thing seems.

"The mental health services," Raul answers immediately. "Not just drug counseling, but actually getting these guys therapists who can listen to them talk about what they've been through and where they're going."

For now, Raul will play that role too.

RAUL TAKES ME TO BOYLE HEIGHTS in his new Toyota Corolla— spotlessly clean inside and out. He wants me to see where he grew up.

Instead, he shows me what has replaced where he grew up. Like so many urban neighborhoods considered high-crime areas, Pico Gardens and Aliso Village were razed and rebuilt to accommodate a more mixed-income population. The U.S. Department of Housing and Urban Development granted $50 million to fund the rebuilding in the mid-1990s. Today it looks more like a condominium complex for retirees—coral-colored, rosebushes everywhere, the occasional old woman hobbling by with arms full of groceries. As we walk around, I tell Raul that I'm a little stunned.

"When I hear 'projects,' I think towering, drab high-rises," I admit, picturing the projects I've worked at in Harlem or the ones up the street from my apartment in Brooklyn.

"Well, it was never quite like that, L.A.-style, you know. But still, this isn't anything like it used to be," Raul admits. He seems conflicted. On the one hand, he's happy that the neighborhood is cleaner. There's a community garden, playgrounds for the kids, even a basketball court and rec center that the city commissioned him to help plan. His mother still lives in the complex, an American flag waving peacefully outside her window.

On the other hand, he does seem to miss the old vibe— loud music, a consistent buzz of adolescent energy, the constant threat of violence that made the whole neighborhood feel electric. Raul tells me about one of his high school teachers, a Holocaust survivor, who once said that people in public housing "live like dogs." She compared it to the living conditions in the concentration camps—quarters so close that people were naturally drawn into fighting. At first he'd been offended. "Fuck you," he told her and stormed out of the classroom.

"Years later," he admits, "I realized what she was saying. There was no room to breathe here before. It made people crazy." Of course, it's not that the violence has entirely stopped. Boyle Heights is still considered gang infested and teeming with at-risk kids—many of whom Raul has counseled at one point or another.

The first catalyst for his formal work with youth was the summer of '94, when seven people, one of them only twelve years old, were killed in Pico-Aliso. Raul, nineteen at the time, and his friend Carlos decided to start an after-school program in response to what they called "the massacre of '94." The 4-H organization, usually thought of as a rural program, was actually looking to help out after hearing about the unprecedented violence. They provided a small amount of funding for snacks, sports equipment, and the equivalent of a janitor's salary for Raul and Carlos.

There was an empty gym near the projects that the Catholic Archdiocese of Los Angeles owned but hadn't yet figured out what to do with, so it rented the space to Raul for a dollar a year. He went to East Los Angeles Community College during the day—studying political science—then he opened the doors of the gym around 2:00 p.m. and gave the kids activities to keep them busy, helped them with their homework, and talked to them about their struggles. They held poetry nights, painted murals over gang tags, and celebrated holidays together. "No one was dealing with the wannabes at that time," Raul says. Only the hard-core gang members were getting the attention of authorities or community intervention. Raul saw his role as that of prevention—get the kids just before the gangs would recruit them.

Raul was known for his audaciousness. He would ask full-fledged gangbangers to donate drug money for Easter egg hunts and movie nights for the "little homies." If he caught wind that two of his students were beefing and rumor was escalating about an impending fight, he would take them into the empty parking lot, check them for weapons, and then encourage them to have it out right there and then. "They were going to do it anyway," Raul explains sheepishly. "I'm sure I could have gotten in a lot of trouble for that, but at least that way I knew the violence wouldn't escalate. Handle it old school, and then I can take someone to get medical care if they need it." Raul himself was known to show up at apartments of kids who came to the after-school program with black eyes and bruises and give abusive fathers a taste of their own medicine.

Perhaps Raul's most ballsy move took place during the volatile winter of 1995. He insisted that the kids from two different turfs were going to celebrate Christmas together with a big pizza party. Many people from Pico-Aliso thought he was nuts to bring teenagers from separate sides—kids with older brothers and sisters deep in rival gangs (Cuatro Flats and TMC were the big ones)—into the same room and expect them not to rip one another apart. But Raul was insistent.

The negative energy was palpable. Within the first few minutes, a kid reported to Raul that someone had tagged on the bathroom wall. Thirteen-, fourteen-, and fifteen-year-old kids in oversized T-shirts and sagging pants stood posted up on opposite sides of the room, staring one another down, imitating their older siblings to a T. The pizza steamed from the dozen boxes sitting on the front table.

Raul announced, "No one is eating any pizza until every single one of you goes into that bathroom and does your part to paint over the tagging. Some people don't think you all are capable of spending time in one room. They think you all are animals. But I know better. You know better." One by one, the kids trickled out and took the paintbrush that Raul had set near the gang symbol, dipped it in white paint, and erased the false start. The celebration was a success, at least temporarily—leading to friendships and even romances cross-neighborhood.

As Raul and I walk through Pico Gardens, he tells the story with pride, but also a lot of sadness. "Fifteen years later, I've lost six of those kids who were sitting around that table eating pizza together," he says. "They all killed each other."

"How do you handle that?" I ask.

"Not very well sometimes." We stand in front of a mural that he helped raise money for, a beautiful painting of the cityscape at night, and he tells me about Richard, his most painful loss. Richard had been a regular at the after-school program, and Raul would often pull him aside and mentor him. He'd known Richard since he was a baby. "I can still remember that little homie breast-feeding!" Raul says. Richard didn't always steer completely clear of trouble, but for the most part he managed to keep his nose clean.

One celebratory evening, Raul ended up at a graduation party where Richard, all grown up at twenty-two years old, was also hanging out. "It was an emotional night," Raul says. "Carlos and I were drinking with the fools we used to buy snacks for. Leo, one of them, had just gotten back from a study abroad in South America and was graduating from Chico State. Richard had graduated from high school a few years ago and was thinking about refocusing and getting into college." It dawned on Raul that all the work they'd done those years ago to keep kids off the streets had paid off.

Richard and Raul were standing on a back patio, drinking some beers and talking about a nice-looking girl nearby. "I think she's staring at you," Raul teased Richard.

"Shut up, fool! She's grown up. That's a lady," Richard said.

"Shut up, punk, she's just twenty-six," Raul responded, laughing at Richard's shyness. He wandered over to the pretty girl and struck up a conversation.

But the mood shifted from light to dark in a matter of seconds. Richard tapped Raul on the shoulder and said, "This fool is tripping with us." When Raul turned around, he could feel the tension of a fight brewing. As a stranger approached, Raul said, "Hey man, be cool. We're just chillin' right here." But it was too late—tempers were flaring beyond reason.

Raul doesn't remember what happened next. Some people have told him that he took a swing at the guy first, then knocked him over an ice chest nearby. Others have said that the guy initiated the fight, and then one of his friends came around the corner with a bottle and hit Raul over the head. In any case, Raul woke up a few minutes later with half of his body in a Jacuzzi and his head hot with spilled blood. "I could see people's legs running away from me in all directions."

A girl at the party helped Raul to his feet and walked him into the house, taking him to the bathroom, where she helped him get out of his shirt and lean over the tub to wash the blood off his head. As the cool water ran over his hot face, Raul heard more commotion out front. He rushed out of the bathroom and out the front door. Richard was standing in the street, and when he saw Raul he shouted, "Carlos is fighting with that fool over there! He has a gun!"

Raul inched his way closer to get a better look, leaning on a shiny black car. When he looked back, Richard was gone. "Damn, where did he go?" he remembers thinking. And then there were two distinct gunshots, and Raul heard Leo's disembodied voice from somewhere yelling for him: "Raul, they shot Richard! They shot Rats!"

Raul ran back to where he'd seen Richard just moments ago and found him leaning back in Leo's arms, eyes half-mast. He'd been shot in the back, but the bullet didn't go through. A little bump on his chest marked where it was lodged. As Raul knelt beside him, Richard looked up and asked his mentor for one last favor: "Take care of me, Rulies."

The experience absolutely shattered Raul. "I never wanted to love a kid again," he reflects, rubbing his shoe in the dirt. Richard died of internal bleeding. Raul himself had to get stitches and four new teeth (the bottle to the head cracked his bottom teeth at the root), and he suffered a severe concussion. He quit work, shaved his head, and went down to Mexico for a while to stay with some extended family and friends. But even in a little village in Mexico, he couldn't escape: "I ended up staying across from this school for a while. Same kids, different faces."

Referring to Father Greg Boyle, Celeste Fremon writes:

For Greg there is no distance, no film of protection. He cares for the gang members as if they were literally his own children. Certainly it is Greg's offer of unconditional love that is the source of magic. But what happens if you give your heart to ten dozen kids, many of whom will die violently and young, the rest of whom are dying slow deaths of the spirit?

"Burnout is the cost, I think," Greg says quietly.

When Raul came back to L.A., he ran into Father Greg on the street and sought his wisdom. "I don't know what to do," Raul told him. "I don't know if I can continue doing this work, but I really want to, because it means a lot to me."

Father Greg gave him a knowing look and replied, "Sometimes you have to go into a different field. Sometimes it's time to get away, time to go somewhere else."

Raul was crushed. "I took it like, 'Wow, he says I can't take this type of work no more.' I felt like my mentor was telling me to give up."

In retrospect, Raul realizes that he's actually grateful for Father Greg's advice. "I have to thank him for telling me that, because if it wasn't for that conversation, I probably would have come back and made my life even more miserable. I wouldn't have been able to give the guys the attention they deserve."

Instead, Raul tried a traditional job. One of his former students said that her boyfriend would hire Raul as a semitruck dispatcher. He would make almost twice as much as he'd ever made counseling kids, but he had a hard time learning the code that the truck drivers used, and he hated sitting all day. He tried filing instead, but three months of that also grew monotonous. Raul was depressed, even suicidal. "I was crying in my girlfriend's arms every Saturday morning for two, three months," he says. "Then I quit and basically became the grim reaper. I'd sleep all day and then come out at night, looking for a fight. Everyone knew something was up with me. I was drinking too much. Mad at the world. Friends would say, 'Dog, you're trippin'. You need help.'"

One day, at the peak of desperation, Raul ran to the historic Fourth Street Bridge, which stretches over the Los Angeles River. He looked up at the San Gabriel Mountains. He looked down at the river, flowing with a vengeance that day. He thought about jumping in and being free of his burden forever. "I was thinking of Richard so much," he says. "I don't want to say that it was Richard's voice, you know, that said 'Rulies, go back and finish what you were doing,' but I don't really have any other explanation. I just felt this shift where I knew I couldn't die."

Reluctantly, Raul admits, "It sounds crazy, but I'm pretty sure that he was there. Richard knew that I saved his life for a long time, and he wanted to save mine."

Raul had a second, very unlikely, angel. One day as he was climbing the stairs in a building known for being the home to many hard-core gang members, one of them stopped him, looked deep into his eyes, and said, "You don't belong here. It's not that I don't like you. You've taken care of a lot of little homies, but you're going backward. You're confused. You're not like us, Rulies."

That gangbanger would end up with a life sentence for murder. Raul would end up pulling himself out of his depression by reconnecting with Father Boyle and getting back into the work at Homeboy Industries.

Raul and I walk by the old lot where they used to run the after-school program, and he points out a tree looming high above the fence and casting a shadow on the street below. "We planted that tree!" he exclaims, for the moment pulled away from a dark place. "We planted a bunch of them, actually, but there's only a few that survived."

"Do you believe in heaven and hell and all that?" I ask.

"I don't believe in hell." He pauses, looking down and taking a deep breath, then goes on: "Hell is what we're living in right now. A place where fathers molest their young sons and daughters, where kids I fed get killed by other kids I fed. Fuck, if this isn't fucking hell, what is?"

We walk a couple more blocks to the original Dolores Mission Church, where Raul used to hang out as a small child and where his mom still goes to services every Sunday at 6:00 p.m. It's a small church, stocky and humble in orange stucco. It's closed, but we peek through the windows, and I imagine Raul there as a little boy—sweeping up, wiping the pews down with a rag, cleaning the votive holders with their stubborn wax—and his community's whispered prayers.

BACK AT HOMEBOY INDUSTRIES, we walk into the cramped office that Raul shares with the two other caseworkers. He introduces me to Matt, a Jesuit volunteer who recently graduated from Boston College (a dead ringer for Ashton Kutcher, but bright blond), and Arturo, one of Raul's clients. "This is my sister from Mexico," Raul deadpans.

They both look at me with squinty eyes and then burst out laughing. "Shut up, Rulies," Matt says, flicking Raul in the shoulder.

"You up on those case notes?" Raul asks.

"That's what I was just about to do," Matt says, flipping open the laptop. Raul oversees Matt and one other caseworker out of this tiny office. There's a big metal desk and file cabinet along one tan wall, with a desktop computer and a few books. Along the other wall is a loveseat, and the third has a chair. It's eclectically decorated with a baseball calendar, a framed photo of a giant-cheeked baby girl that says I LOVE YOU DADDY! across the bottom, the DASH bus schedule, two black-and-white prints of a group of kids on a hiking trip—Raul smiling triumphantly in the center—and a red and black plaster mask. "What's that?" I ask Raul, motioning toward the mask.

"Guys in here walk around with masks all day. That's there to remind them to take it off when they're in here with me," he answers.

Arturo, a tall guy with broad shoulders, hands Raul a letter from a firefighter training school he's attending. "I need boots, dog," he tells Raul. Arturo wears very dark glasses that wrap around his bald head. When he has to remove them in class, he's mortified, as he has a mean raccoon tan. He just finished his bid for murder a few months ago. He's been incarcerated since the age of twelve, and before that, he and his eight brothers and sisters were shuffled between foster homes—abandoned by their mother, who had a drug problem.

When he first got out of prison, he had nowhere to go. Raul picked him up and took him to McDonald's, but Arturo was too paranoid to stand in line around a lot of people, convinced one of them might take him out. Raul brought him to his mom's house instead. When they walked in, Guadalupe gave Arturo a big hug, as she did every one of her son's companions (whether friend, client, or coworker). Arturo didn't let go for a long time.

She made him chorizo, beans, and eggs, which he devoured in seconds.

As Raul was driving Arturo to a hotel room that he'd secured for him until he could find his own place, Arturo looked over and asked, "Why do you care about me so much?"

"Honestly, Arturo," Raul responded, "you remind me of a lot of the youngsters I've known." Arturo was exactly as old as Richard would have been, had he survived.

There is no mistaking one of Raul's most valuable assets as a social worker: his clients are his brothers. He is from the neighborhood in which he works. He knows the smell of the kitchens there, the texture of the asphalt, the specific language of loyalty and heartbreak that is completely unique to the boys of East L.A. Raul has a deep knowing—so deep as to be invisible to him—that informs his work every single day.

Raul speaks of Father Greg with only the highest esteem, but it's hard not to notice the biggest contrast between them. Father Greg may be a veteran immigrant in the war-torn nations of Pico and Aliso, but he is not a native. When I ask Raul about this difference, he thoughtfully responds, "I know the people. I know the deep internal soul struggle and how we deal with it. No doubt Father Greg is familiar with this type of stuff, because everyone talks to him. But it's like me saying, 'I know what it's like to live in a big house with a big swimming pool and a view of the ocean.' I've been invited to homes like that before, but to say I know what it's like to wake up in the middle of the night and look out at the ocean, it's just impossible.

"Father Greg is very familiar with the obstacles. Emotionally and spiritually, he has a slight idea of what it's like. But he can never really know."

BACK IN THE OFFICE, Raul barely looks up from the papers he's shuffling. "What kind of boots you need?" he asks. Arturo lifts the office phone off the cradle and starts dialing a number. "If I call them, you'll talk to them?" he asks Raul.

"No, fool. You're going to figure this out. Now sit down at the computer and Google them," Raul responds.

Arturo sits down, visibly uncomfortable. "We can just order them like that? So I just type up the name of the boots?" He tentatively types the name of the boots in the Google box in the navigation bar, peck by peck. A long list of search results comes up.

"Now click on that one with the blue letters," Raul explains.

"Man, I hate looking dumb," Arturo says under his breath as he studies the Web page.

"You know I don't like helping you, dog," Raul reminds him. Thirty minutes go by. I have to physically restrain myself from getting up and aiding Arturo. Watching him nervously click on search items, painstakingly type in keywords, and get overwhelmed makes me feel like I could jump out of my skin. Raul seems unfazed. "Keep searching, big guy," he encourages Arturo. "See how good it feels to do good work for yourself?"

Forty-five minutes later, Arturo finally finds a place twenty minutes away that carries the right boots. He calls the store to find out how much they're charging. In the middle of the call, his girlfriend phones his cell. "Hold on, okay, baby?" he says, dropping the cell to the desk and resuming his fact-finding mission. He asks the store clerk, "Is there any discount for firefighters? I'm gonna be one."

Then Matt eggs Arturo on: "Why don't you ask her if there's a discount for being attractive?"

"Um, excuse me, miss, what if I'm fine?" Arturo says, smiling mischievously. We all burst out laughing. Then he looks down and realizes that his cell is lying open on the desk, his girlfriend listening to every flirtatious word. "Oh, fuck!" he screams and picks it up. "Baby, I'm sorry," he pleads, walking out of the cramped office to find some privacy. The three of us laugh so hard we cry.

———

HOMEBOY INDUSTRIES IS BUZZING the next morning. Raul debriefs me on what's already gone down in the thirty minutes he's been at work. There have been three deportations. Raul is trying to get some money secured so that one boy can fly home to his village once he's dropped off in Tijuana. One of Raul's clients got into a car accident the day before—not actually his fault, but he has no car insurance, so Raul is going to help him find the cheapest kind online so he can present it retroactively. One of the pregnant girls on staff doesn't have food in her house, so Raul is figuring that out. All of the pregnant girls have been ordered to stop wearing tight jeans. Arturo is breathing down his neck for the fire boots, so he'll drive him out to get them later in the afternoon.

Another kid has suddenly grown paranoid of another caseworker—"What are you, a cop?" he asks when Matt checks in to see how he's doing (a completely normal practice at Homeboy Industries). The kid was caught masturbating in one of the classrooms and seems especially reserved. Raul sat down with him first thing and asked, "Did you shoot someone?" "No." "Did you rob someone?" "No." "Did you get a girl pregnant?" "No." "Did you have sex with a young girl?" "No." "Do you want to see a therapist?" "Yes." Raul phoned downstairs and made an appointment for him.

"How did you know to come on so strong?" I ask, surprised that Raul would ask such direct questions.

He shrugs and says, "Don't know. Just seemed like the right way to snap him out of it and make sure he knows that we're noticing him acting strange and that we've seen it all before."

"So what do you think might be going on with him?"

"Maybe his girlfriend broke up with him. They always think they can handle it, but when a girl leaves them, they lose it. Breaking up is like kryptonite to every guy in here." I'm reminded of all the times over our last few days together when Raul told me about a gang fight that began because of a girl.

"Thursdays are always hard," Raul says, "because people are starting to get nervous about the weekend. I never know what I'm going to have to face on Monday." He looks exhausted and tender, and I think of something I read in *G-Dog and the Homeboys*: Father Boyle admits, "I sort of pray that there's not another death. Or if deaths are inevitable that there's some, I don't know, lead time. Because the deaths get more painful rather than less. You get more vulnerable and fragile, rather than less."

Raul looks at his watch and then says, "Oh shit, I've got a meeting right now about the new grant we're trying to get." The one he's currently running ends in June.

"Can I tag along?" I ask.

"Why not?" he says, shrugging, and we head upstairs to the chief operating officer's corner office. In addition to the COO, a very refined Latina lady in her forties with a chignon, sitting on a giant red exercise ball, there are two other administrators present—a grant writer with orange, princess-like hair, and Mario, the supervisor of case management, who wears an electric-blue button-down and writes detailed notes with a pencil. It's incongruous to see Raul in this formal meeting—he's the opposite of a bureaucrat in every way. He sits down and opens his red leather notebook, which is filled with mostly illegible case notes, phone numbers, and random thoughts.

There's a new RFP (request for proposal) out for job readiness interventions with parolees. It provides a hefty amount of funding for a caseload of twenty-five over the course of a year—easy money to Raul, who is used to having three times that many clients.

After the three discuss the logistics for about ten minutes, the COO looks at Raul. "Any red flags, Rulies?"

"Can we pay for the job training?" he asks. "I'm going to have a real hard time recruiting guys to do this program if we can't pay them. They get out, and they immediately need some income to pay rent and all that."

"We can pay them," the grant writer assures him, looking over the fifty-plus-page RFP, which she has highlighted and scrawled notes on.

"And do we have to report it to their parole officer if they don't show up? We had that come up with another grant, and we got a bad rep in Chino for a while because we're telling the guys, 'Hey, this is voluntary,' but then they get in trouble if they don't show up."

"We define success here, so I don't think we have any obligation to report their attendance to the parole officer," Mario responds.

"We're going to have you lead this up, Rulies," the COO tells him with a very serious face. She asks the grant writer, "There aren't any education stipulations, are there?"

"They want a BA," she says, flipping to that section of the document. Everyone gets a little stiff.

"Usually they'll make an exception for someone who's worked in the field for a long time," Mario says, peeking over her shoulder.

"Oh, yeah, here it is. 'Or commensurate experience.'"

"Cool," Raul says, looking down at his phone, which has been buzzing with text messages all meeting.

It doesn't surprise me that Raul runs into this kind of thinking on the part of grant makers. Too often foundations, government agencies, and even private philanthropists apply classist standards to grassroots organizations. Getting caught up in the number of advanced degrees on a staff, rather than looking at the quality of the work being done, is like evaluating a meal based on the chef's culinary background, not the taste of the food (which is also something that people concerned with status might very well do). Of course there have to be checks and balances, but having educational requirements for work that is largely based on human interaction and cultural understanding is bogus. After all, there is no honorary degree for those who have lived and worked in these communities for years. I just hope that as Homeboy Industries continues to grow, it isn't hampered by the idiot demands of bureaucracy.

When the meeting is adjourned, Raul says, "Courtney, I never finished my degree," as if he is confessing to Father Boyle. "That's one of my goals. I want that diploma. Actually, I want a PhD."

"In what?"

"Social psychology." It's hard to imagine Raul—the bender of rules, the negotiator of compromises, the center of drama—buckling down long enough to survive the bureaucracy of academia.

"Have you ever thought about going to divinity school? Doing what Father Boyle does?" I ask.

"I like women too much," he says, smiling.

AFTER OUR FIRST DAY of interviews together, Raul texts me, "Thanks for listening." I'm touched. I spend so much time worrying about the invasive nature of my profession—dropping into people's lives, demanding their stories—that I sometimes forget that it can be healing and honoring for people as well. It occurs to me that our interaction is probably the first time that Raul has really told his story out loud, at least in this depth.

Months later we chat on the phone, and he updates me on the community at Homeboy. One of the junior staff members was shot and killed over the weekend by his own best friend—high on drugs and humiliation after he lost in a playful wrestling match. The community is devastated. This kid had kids of his own—eight-month-old twins. He was known for his sense of humor and being an important symbol of leadership for the African American population at Homeboy. I can hear the pain in Raul's voice, the same tone he had while talking about losing Richard. "I'm trying to be strong for everyone," he says. "Some people are taking it really hard around here."

"What about you?" I ask.

He laughs quietly. "I don't have time to think about me. I'll deal with it later." Raul is planning on visiting the girlfriend of the deceased and making sure she has enough money to get by, and he is running daily meetings at Homeboy intended to help people deal with their grief by verbalizing what they're feeling rather than retaliating.

"Do you ever think about going to therapy, Raul?" I ask.

"I've thought about it a lot," he admits, "but it scares me, Courtney. I think I'd be like that guy in *Green Mile*, where all this nasty stuff just comes up. I don't want to give this to anybody."

RAUL SOMETIMES LEADS MEDITATIONS with groups in prison, alongside Father Michael Kennedy, another Jesuit priest associated with Homeboy Industries. As we drive to lunch, Raul tells me about the fifteen-minute practice, which he obviously digs a lot. "We start by telling them to get comfortable, close their eyes and all of that, just breathe normally. And then we ask them, 'Imagine the happiest day of your life.'"

"So what's yours?" I interrupt.

"Wow, Courtney. Turning it back on me," he says, laughing, then continues: "I think this one day when I brought a group of the guys to the mountains to go hiking. We were sitting around, eating lunch, and one of the kids and I left and climbed to the top of this hill. There were just miles of green out in front of us when we got up there, miles of space. It was so beautiful. And we sat side by side, and out of nowhere he said, 'Man, I love you more than my father.'" Raul chokes up and, though he's wearing dark sunglasses, I know he's started crying.

"That was probably my best day."

Recovery Mission
Maricela Guzman, veterans' activist,
Los Angeles

Maricela Guzman, twenty-one, was dressed in a clean, pressed Navy uniform as she paced around the empty hallway well past midnight. Her heavy-soled footsteps echoed, though she was small—five foot three and in great shape after all the prep for boot camp. She was officially "standing watch"—in Navy fantasyland, guarding her ship from outside intruders; in reality, enduring hours of mind-numbing silence in the moonlit hallways of a dormitory in Great Lakes, Illinois. All Navy recruits had to do it, ostensibly for practice, probably to increase their vulnerability. Maricela's eyelids threatened to drop closed at any second.

She tried to keep herself awake by imagining the maps pinned on her bedroom wall back home in South Central L.A. She would lie on her bed so she could stare at the blue-green expanses of foreign lands—Africa was her favorite—and dream about going there. She'd memorize the capital cities and names of the countries. She'd never even been on a plane. She repeated some of the countries she could remember in her head: "Mali, Ghana, Senegal . . ."

Suddenly a body burst from nowhere and grabbed her from behind, covering her neck with one sweaty hand and her mouth with the other. If only it were some kind of drill. Instead it was reality. Before Maricela could process what was happening to her, the attacker dragged her into the darkened stairwell and was clawing at the standard-issue black leather belt on her pants. She never saw his face as he raped her, but the chest of his uniform clearly indicated that he was a Recruit Division Commander—a superior officer. The fact that the light had been turned off in this section of stairwell meant that the attack had been premeditated. It was Maricela's first sexual experience.

"THE PERSON I WAS at that time died," Maricela, now thirty-two, says at our first meeting. She stares at the brown napkin on the table between us and draws sharp lines in succession with her pen. She's wearing black wide-legged pants, sneakers, and a brown zip-up jacket that dwarfs her small frame. Her jet-black hair is pulled back in a no-nonsense bun. Her skin is a pale brown, her lips purple and full. She is beautiful, and she also radiates profound exhaustion.

"What did you do after you were attacked?" I ask, tentatively. I'm scared of pushing for any details she doesn't immediately volunteer.

"I can't talk about that yet," she answers, looking up with icy eyes. She doesn't look angry, but completely shut down. "I'm still working on that in therapy." And then she reaches into her purse and pulls out a Prozac pill. "Speaking of therapy," she says, eyebrows raised, and washes it down with tea.

Maricela was not initially comfortable with the idea of going to therapy at all. It certainly wasn't talked about openly in the Navy, and her family—working-class Mexican immigrants—saw therapy as something that only "crazy people" do. It was other female veterans that first convinced her to try it out.

Much of Maricela's healing, in fact, has revolved around finding a community of women who have endured the same military culture, and in a lot of cases, the same kind of sexual violation. Along with fourteen other women, she founded the Service Women's Action Network (SWAN) in 2007, whose mission is "to improve the welfare of U.S. servicewomen and all women veterans." Its vision statement explains that "SWAN advocates for servicewomen and women veterans by educating the public, recommending sound policy reform to legislators, developing creative, healing and empowering community programs, offering personal support and guidance from fellow women veterans and providing pro bono legal referrals from military law experts."

Maricela refuses to take on a paid role with SWAN, because she believes it will taint her relationship to the work. Instead she volunteers her time to connect women veterans whom she meets in her travels to the SWAN network so they can get help navigating the veterans' benefits system, legal advice, and much-needed solidarity with other women who have been through the military experience.

SWAN could not have formed at a more crucial moment for women in the military—just as 155,000 women were serving in Afghanistan and Iraq, twenty-six times as many as served in Vietnam. Helen Benedict, author of *The Lonely Soldier: The Private War of Women Serving in Iraq*, reports that "by September 2008, 592 American female soldiers had been wounded in action and 102 had died in Iraq, more than in the Korean, Vietnam, first Gulf, and Afghanistan wars combined." According to the Department of Veterans Affairs, women currently make up 15 percent of the total military.

But even more crucial is the fact that in the last few years the nation has finally been waking up to the astronomically high rate of military sexual assault. Though it isn't a new problem, there is a new consciousness of its prevalence. Major media outlets—from the *New York Times* to Salon.com—are finally reporting on it. In response to public outrage, the Defense Department created the Sexual Assault Prevention and Response Office in 2005. Benedict reports that one in three women serving in the military are sexually attacked by comrades and that "harassment is virtually universal."

Hearing these statistics, as shocking as they are, is still an abstract experience for the average civilian. But sitting across from Maricela, looking into her dark eyes as she explains what she's been through, makes it painfully real. It's as if Maricela's military experiences, her rape especially, have altered her DNA. She's spent the last ten years trying to recover her old self, or at least integrate the new Maricela—wounded but resilient, angry as hell, exhausted but inexhaustible, understandably dark—with the old Maricela. After our first meeting, I sit in my rental car and cry for a few minutes before turning on the engine.

A COUPLE OF BULKY VIDEO CAMERAS record footage of Maricela, looking more like an insurance sales rep—boxy brown suit and matching pumps—than a veterans' activist. She stands resolutely in front of a lectern and speaks in soft non sequiturs, obviously nervous: "To this day the VA [U.S. Department of Veterans Affairs] has not honored my claim for posttraumatic stress disorder. In 2004 I tried suicide. The reason I'm here today is to make sure that other women are healed. If my story helps other women, then I hope that's the case. Because one life cannot . . . my life was almost stolen, and I need to make sure that other lives are saved."

SWAN has been invited to participate in a congressional roundtable hosted by the House Committee on Veterans' Affairs called "The Growing Needs of Women Veterans: Is the VA Ready?" Held about a week before Memorial Day, the roundtable is intended to explore some of the issues facing women veterans who try to access health care. SWAN, which has been feverishly working on a solid strategic plan and redesigning its Web site, is treating this opportunity like a bit of a coming-out party.

Eli Painted Crow, Maricela's mentor, stands nearby, dressed in a Western-patterned blazer, a brown bandana tied flat and tight across her forehead, and big silver rings on almost every finger. Her face is set in a grimace, as if she can hardly stand being in the hallowed halls of federal power.

Only a fraction of the crew is in attendance, but it still feels like a family reunion. Maricela has flown in from Los Angeles, along with Julianne, the media director of SWAN and a police officer with the LAPD. Anu, the executive director of SWAN, has come down from New York, along with Jen, the associate director, and Rachel, the legal advisor. Kehontas, who moonlights as a barber, is the financial director, and she flew in from Louisville. Eli came in from Tucson. With the exception of Rachel, who is doing pro bono work for SWAN, all of them are veterans.

When the press conference is over we all head down the hall for the big event. Maricela is off the hook here. SWAN's executive director, Anu, will do the testifying at the actual roundtable.

The large room is already filled with congressional aides milling around in skirt suits, with BlackBerry smartphones and cups of Starbucks coffee in their hands. Twenty women—most of them in their fifties and sixties, and all of them working for women veterans' advocacy groups—sit around one end of the square of long tables covered with pristine white tablecloths and microphones. Anu takes her seat at the table of honor, and the rest of SWAN finds a line of chairs nearby to settle into.

Anu, like Maricela, fits in—she's worn a black pant suit and exudes a sort of benign professionalism. But Jen and Kehontas proudly sport an alternative style—they're dressed in boots and men's blazers; Jen's got a piercing and a big mane of wavy, untamed hair, and Kehontas has barely any, making the tattoos on her neck totally visible. With them and permanently stoic Eli, the SWAN crew stands out against the gilded frames and Ann Taylor pant suits.

One woman sitting with the aides shouts, "We should get a picture of all these women in this room!" A few other aides giggle. Four or five senators—a couple of them men—settle into their seats at the table behind wooden placards with their names on them. It appears that three-fourths of the official committee hasn't bothered to show up. Congressman Bob Filner, the head of the committee, begins the discussion with the obvious: "The VA of the twenty-first century must meet the needs of all veterans."

The advocates seated around the table are invited to give short remarks on what they see as the most pressing problems facing women veterans and to make recommendations for how these problems can be fixed. Anu is the second to speak. She testifies:

> The last place many survivors of MST [military sexual trauma] want to go for treatment or counseling is a VA hospital. My first trip to the Manhattan VA Hospital was a nightmare. I felt like I was running a gauntlet as I stepped into the lobby and was confronted by a sea of hostile faces, all of them male.

Maricela nods her head vigorously. She's spoken often about the experience of being retraumatized by unfriendly security guards, staff, and other patients at VA centers. Anu goes on, the anger barely but unmistakably detectable underneath her very clear, dignified presentation:

> Most veterans and VA employees assume women veterans are secretaries, wives, or cleaning staff. . . . The first psychiatrist I saw rolled his eyes at me when I told him I needed to talk to a female doctor. The MST counselor was too overbooked to take me on as a patient. A physician was so shocked that I had been a Marine that he told me I looked like a "shopkeeper."

45

To add insult to injury, despite the detailed evidence I submitted supporting service-connected trauma from MST, including witness statements, the VA rejected my claim.

After she finishes, there a few moments of stunned silence, and then Filner says, "We've got a big job."

"Yes, you do," Anu replies matter-of-factly.

Throughout the rest of the hearing, which lasts for two hours, Maricela and the others scribble furious notes with statistics and policy arguments and drop them in front of Anu.

Congressman Tim Walz, who repeatedly refers to the veterans—both those present and in general—as "warriors," is red with anger. "Are you telling me, I mean is there consensus among you, that no progress has been made with regard to sexual assault?" he asks, looking around with pleading eyes.

The entire table of women—veterans from Operation Iraqi Freedom, Vietnam, the Gulf War, and even World War II (Josephine Anton, ninety-three years old, sits tiny and proud at the table, a blue hat decorated with Women's Army Corps pins and medals of honor atop her head)—nod their heads in unison, a few letting an emphatic "yes" escape their lips.

"That's tragic," Walz says, shaking his head. "Just tragic."

Filner adds, "It reminds me of something Dr. Martin Luther King said. 'I can't make a man love me, but I sure as hell'—he didn't say sure as hell—'can prevent him from lynching me.'" (The actual quotation is: "It may be true that the law cannot make a man love me, but it can keep him from lynching me, and I think that's pretty important.")

These two men are having genuine emotion, and it is indeed refreshing. But there is something incongruent about hearing all of these statistics and experiences spoken in calm and official tones in a fancy room with chandeliers and grandfather clocks, when we're really talking about women being assaulted, their uniforms ripped, their underwear filled with blood, their faces smeared with dirt and tears. We're talking about violent acts characterized by a mess of anger, humiliation, and bodily fluids—the polar opposite of this pristine old room with its sanctimonious airs. We're talking about violations that mark the moment when women become unrecognizable to themselves, when their sense of safety is obliterated, when their lives are forever changed.

Maricela shakes her head and doodles on the VA pamphlets in front of her. She looks out the window as if she wants to escape. I feel a swell of anger rise up in me. While I'm glad that Congressmen Filner and Walz are connecting to the issue on an emotional level, another part of me is infuriated. They are so late to this outrage, as if it's all a big shock to them; anyone who serves on the Committee on Veterans' Affairs should know that sexual assault in the military is rampant.

And even more important, I sense that their notion of what needs to be done is woefully inadequate. Essentially, they will entertain the notion that legislation or VA policy needs to change, but the idea that military culture needs a fundamental overhaul is beyond the scope of their imaginations. They're willing to try to keep military men from raping their sisters in arms—a kind of gender-based, psychological "lynching"—but they can't make any promises about convincing men to respect women. They want their "bad guys"—just like in Abu Ghraib—rather than recognizing that dehumanization is inextricable from the military system itself. In the end, they get the catharsis of their own outrage without actually doing anything fundamental to prevent the next Maricela from being raped.

MARICELA GUZMAN'S PARENTS—Maria and José—could never have imagined that their daughter would one day testify in the hallowed halls of Congress. They immigrated to the United States from Mexico illegally, in 1974 and 1976 respectively. Maricela was born in Los Angeles in 1977. Until she was twelve, her family of six (four siblings came after her) lived crammed into a studio apartment in Koreatown. Maria worked in a makeup factory (and, later, in factories that made airplane and toilet parts). José worked in a fancy hotel in Century City. In fact, he still works there, having shown up and sprayed the dishes clean for thirty-two years now.

When she was eleven, Maricela's parents got U.S. residency through an amnesty program. When she was thirteen, the whole family moved to their first bona fide home in South Central L.A. (Incidentally, this was right after the infamous L.A. riots, so racial tension was still high.) Maricela, the best English speaker in the family, filled out all of the paperwork for what would turn out to be a ghastly high-interest mortgage. Three years later, in danger of losing the house, she dropped out of high school and started working in the neighborhood McDonald's to help the family.

She saved the house, but missed school, where she'd always excelled. At eighteen, the finances back under control, she returned and got her high school diploma while still working part-time at McDonald's. At twenty-one she started at East Los Angeles Community College. She was determined to be the first person in her family to graduate from college. Her father never went to school past the age of five, and her mother dropped out after third grade to start working.

When Maria insisted on looking for a second job so she could help her daughter pay for school, Maricela was devastated. The last thing she wanted to see was either of her parents working any harder. Even so, Maricela *was* starting to falter under the grind—she'd wake to the smell of hash browns frying at 4:00 a.m., leave McDonald's at noon to get to school, attend classes until 9:00 p.m., then come home and study while wheeling endlessly on the exercise bike she'd found at a garage sale and placed in the center of her tiny room.

As if intuiting her crumbling resolve, a military recruiter targeted Maricela near the end of her first semester in college, approaching her on campus. "It was a surreal experience," Maricela says. "Within thirty minutes this guy knew my entire life story. It was like he saw through me."

He spoke glowingly about the military experience—how it was a great opportunity to get money for college, see the world, do something noble for the country that had given your parents a better life. According to a 2004 *Boston Globe* report, the Defense Department spends a whopping $2.6 billion each year on recruiting. While many military recruits cite the educational funding as one of their primary reasons for joining up, many recruits never receive any money for college. Many vets return home with mental health issues that prevent them from pursuing academics, some feel sheepish about starting college at an older age, and on top of all that, it is notoriously difficult to navigate the military bureaucracy.

Maricela explains, "It was a way to get out of my neighborhood, a way to see the world, a way to finally be done with my financial worries." She signed on the dotted line without saying a word to anyone in her family.

MARICELA WAS GIDDY the morning she left, excited to be taking her very first flight, curious to finally see what boot camp was like after a summer of anticipating it (she'd signed up in the spring of '98 and left that August). After arriving in Chicago, she was driven with a bunch of other recruits in a bus to Great Lake, Illinois, twenty-five miles away. The intake troops immediately made her dump the contents of her duffle out and send just about everything that might remind her of her former life—her books, soap, shampoo—back home.

The next twenty-four hours were a blur of paperwork, fittings, and mind-numbing waiting. But no sleep. "They're trying to break you down from the very beginning," Maricela says.

At first things went relatively smoothly. She was placed with a gender-mixed group that included a really nice woman with whom she connected instantly. Like Maricela, Debbie was a little bit older than the rest of the group (mostly eighteen-year-olds) and her mother was also an immigrant (from El Salvador).

The workouts were manageable, and Maricela is naturally disciplined, so she didn't mind the rigidity of the routine. The brutality that began after the first two weeks—which were punishment-free while the troops got their bearings—was disconcerting, but she figured that if she flew under the radar, she could avoid any major confrontations. She loved learning, and the military jargon was like a foreign language; she loved calling the bathroom "the head." Even though it felt a little silly to go on watches and write logs when they were all just sleeping in the equivalent of a bunch of dorms in the middle of nowhere, she didn't mind it.

Until that night. And then everything changed. "The night I was raped altered my entire existence," Maricela says. "Suddenly things that had felt easy, felt really challenging. Not just mental things, but physical things too.

"I survived by going silent," Maricela says. "I became completely robotic." You might assume that such a reaction would go unnoticed in the military culture of submission, but there is a fine distinction, Maricela explains, between being obedient and being too silent. Eventually, her blank stare started to stick out.

Her drill sergeant noticed and asked her friend, Debbie—who by that time had taken on a leadership role within the division—"Why is Guzman suddenly so quiet?"

Her friend, not knowing anything about her sexual assault, shrugged and said, "We'll just have to break her down more."

Maricela, always careful not to assign blame, assures me that her friend was just looking out for her: "She didn't have any idea what happened to me, so this was her way of building me up as a soldier."

They began giving her more reps then the rest of her peers—more push-ups, more pull-ups, more laps. Worst of all, they also gave her more watches. The Navy is known for utilizing sleep deprivation to get submission out of their new recruits; little did they know that every watch duty was retraumatizing to increasingly internal Maricela.

Eventually, feeling on the edge of a nervous breakdown, she decided to tell her supervisor. She turned the knob on his office door and opened it, blurting out, "I need to speak with you."

He stood slowly with a menacing look on his face. "Drop and give me twenty." In her haste to finally speak the truth, Maricela had forgotten the appropriate Navy policy for approaching a supervisor—knock on door, stand at attention, request to speak. She did twenty push-ups, tears beginning to fill her eyes.

"Now get up and approach again," he shouted. Maricela stood, but couldn't move. She was frozen. Her supervisor's voice got louder, his tone more enraged: "Do you think I have all day? Drop and give me another twenty." She did. This time the tears fell out of her eyes, splashing on the floor below. She stood.

"You figure out how to do it right now?" he asked, just inches from her face. Again, she couldn't move. "There is a procedure . . ." His words, at this point, became indecipherable to Maricela. It was as if her mind was systematically shutting down, her emotions taking over. Tears streamed down her cheeks. She saw his hand drop, pointing at the floor, and knew to drop and give him another twenty.

When she stood, he stared at her in disgust for a few long seconds and then motioned toward the door. She turned on her heel and walked out. Maricela wouldn't attempt to tell another soul about her rape for eight years.

WHEN MARICELA WAS FOURTEEN years old, she went to Jalisco, Mexico, to take care of her grandmother, who had broken her hip after a fall. Maricela anticipated a quiet summer away from her disruptive brothers and the stress of living in South Central L.A. But when she arrived, rumors were circulating. Apparently her grandmother, one of the elder women of the small community, had been involved in a negotiation over some land, and it had gone awry. People at church—the epicenter of the village—were buzzing about the drama. The minister approached Maricela's *abuela* after service one day and graciously asked her to take a break from her Sunday sojourn for a while, at least until the controversy died down.

Miniature Maricela looked up at the minister and immediately spit back, "This is a house of God! Unless God comes out of the sky and tells us to leave, we're staying. And in fact, we'll sit in the front row."

Clearly, Maricela always had the capacity for righteous anger; but it wasn't until she was stationed on Diego Garcia, starting in March 1999, that she began to develop an activist consciousness. Diego Garcia is an island a thousand miles south of India, home to a joint U.S.-U.K. military base that serves as a naval refueling station. It is also home to the B-52s, B-1s, and B-2s whose fiery bomb drops over Iraq marked the beginning of the invasion on March 22, 2003.

Diego Garcia was also where Maricela met her husband-to-be, Jason (not his real name). On her second day on the island, Maricela heard that an old friend had a really bad sunburn. She brought a special cream that her mother had made for her (since she was also prone to burning because of her light skin) over to her friend's dorm room, and there she set eyes on Jason for the first time. Maricela was still deeply wary of men. She'd had one sexual experience after boot camp, but it had been disappointing. "I only did it because I wanted to replace the abrasive memory of my rape with something else," Marcela says. "But between his lack of experience and my complete disconnect, it didn't really work."

There were four men for every woman on Diego Garcia, so Maricela anticipated feeling like prey. Meeting her husband changed everything. "Jason repelled other men," she says. "They wouldn't mess with me because they knew we were a couple."

It was a whirlwind—romantically and intellectually. Jason, a college boy from a middle-class family in Ohio, was taken by Maricela's beauty—so exotic to him that he actually nicknamed her "jungle girl." (It wasn't until years later that Maricela would realize how offensive she found the nickname.) Maricela found protection, a confidant, and a teacher in Jason. He introduced her to Noam Chomsky and George Orwell. Maricela devoured *Heart of Darkness* by Joseph Conrad and spent long, satisfying hours discussing the ideas with Jason.

The book would become more relevant than they ever could have anticipated, once they started learning about the island's history. Until the 1970s, Diego Garcia was home to two thousand Chagossians, descendants of the Indian workers and African slaves who had been brought to the island centuries earlier. They had no electricity or telephones, but they were peaceful and sustained themselves by growing vegetables and keeping goats, chickens, and pigs. Their economy was largely based on harvesting the local coconuts and extracting their oil for cosmetic companies.

The U.K. government forcibly displaced the native population to Mauritius, a nearby island off the coast of Africa, in 1971, when the U.S. government leased Diego Garcia and decided to build a major military base on it. The Chagossian people have created a movement to fight the British government for their land and ask that the human rights violations they endured be acknowledged, a struggle which continues to this day.

Maricela's research and reading were giving her a totally new way of looking at the world. "All of a sudden I'm looking around, and I realize that the staff on base are being treated like my parents. They're working for slave wages," she says. The U.S. military brings low-wage workers from the Philippines to do the majority of the cooking and cleaning on the island. According to Maricela, they live in shacks and are subjected to a series of dehumanizing rules: they are not allowed to bring a spouse with them (but can bring one child of working-eligible age), they can go home to the Philippines for two weeks once every other year, and they are paid just $240 a month.

Maricela grew completely disillusioned with the military. She was outraged at how it had treated so many poor people of the third world, and she became inspired to talk about it with anyone who would listen. And yet she still wasn't able to name the outrage she felt over her own rape. She didn't tell Jason what had happened to her. His college sweetheart had also been sexually assaulted, and he talked at length about what a huge presence her pain was in their relationship. Maricela didn't want to put him through that again.

But her pain emerged in other ways. They began to fight a lot. "I would get triggered and become really emotionally abusive to him," she says. Maricela would yell and scream, curse at him and call him names. "I'm crazy. I don't know why," she would tell him after their worst fights. "You should leave me."

"It's the military," he would respond. "It's this toxic environment. It will be fine once we leave."

Maricela and Jason married in March 2000 in Los Angeles. Shortly after, they were both stationed in Naples, Italy, where they would stay for the remainder of their service (two and a half years). Maricela thrived in her computer engineering role, finding that workaholism was a fine addiction to keep her from feeling anything—as was booze. She and Jason befriended some radical academics and joined the Green Party back home. They continued to fight mercilessly.

Leading up to June 2002, her discharge date, the officers in her field did everything they could to get her to stay (by this time, she had won multiple awards for her work). But she was sick of being a token—both Latina and female—and determined to go back home to Los Angeles and finish her college degree. She remembers one of her supervisors saying, "You know, twenty to thirty percent of vets never finish college."

"Excuse me, sir, but I will send you my diploma," Maricela replied, and happily left the military behind forever.

MARICELA AND I ARE SITTING across from one another in a sunny booth at Homegirl Café. She is wearing a pink turtleneck sweater, and her hair is pulled taut up top by a headband and hangs long and loose over her shoulders. When I told her that I was interviewing Raul, she was thrilled; not only was she a long-time fan of Homegirl Café's rich coffee, great sandwiches, and laid-back atmosphere, she told me, but she had been thinking about all of the ways in which she'd love to collaborate with Homeboy Industries.

I could hear the voice of an old-school journalism mentor in my head, urging me not to get involved, but the activist in me spoke louder. For the past few days I'd listened to Maricela and Raul speak about their childhoods in L.A., the violence they'd each endured, their parallel journeys of trading one kind of loyalty—militaristic, gang-related—for another—service, hope. I knew I had to get them together. Not only did I see the potential for mutual recognition—always a healing force—but I could imagine all the good they might do for others. Connecting people, it turns out, is part of what I do well.

Raul shows up and graciously asks, "Can I join you?" even though earlier that morning I expressly invited him to come meet Maricela that afternoon.

"Of course," I say, patting the space next to me in the booth. He slides in and Maricela tells him, "I love this place. I was telling Courtney, I bring people here for meetings all the time. I really admire the work that you all do here."

Raul nods and lets a smile creep over his face. "Thanks, thanks."

Maricela goes on to tell him about her work doing counter-recruitment for youth in the area. We have a brief conversation about the difficulty of talking about the dangers of war with groups of teenagers who are surrounded by violence already. "It doesn't make a whole lot of sense to come into communities like these and start using the word 'peace,'" Maricela says. "We know that, so we try to get the kids to think about what violence means to them first."

Raul talks about a friend of his who has just gotten back from a third tour in Iraq and seems mentally unstable. "We all try to avoid talking about his service with him," he says. "We don't want him to blow."

"Sounds like he might have PTSD," Maricela says with a concerned look on her face. "I have it. A lot of veterans do." She begins listing the symptoms of posttraumatic stress disorder—memory loss, lack of sleep, depression, startled reactions . . .

"That sounds like me," Raul says, laughing a little.

Maricela: "Yeah?"

"I went through a really hard time in my life after one of my little homies died, and I basically had all that—couldn't sleep, got real depressed. I used to sit in my house and watch movies over and over and over again. I looked at my collection of DVDs the other day, and I couldn't believe how many I had. I used to drink a lot too."

"Yep, I did that too," Maricela says, nodding. In fact, when Maricela left the military and resettled in Santa Monica with Jason, she found that she couldn't function at all. She couldn't find a job. She couldn't sleep. She couldn't concentrate. She felt "broken." All she could do was watch television, something she'd mostly avoided before her military service.

Raul went on: "I was really violent then. I felt like everyone was out to get me. My homies were just like, 'Whoa, Rulies, you need to chill out. This isn't like you.'"

"Paranoia," Maricela says, "another very common symptom. And just rage in general." For a moment she seems to have been transported elsewhere, her face vacant.

Once in Santa Monica, Jason and Maricela began to get in increasingly physical fights, usually revolving around Maricela's despondency. Jason just didn't understand. He resented her lack of motivation. At one point, he pounded her against a wall by her shoulders so hard that her back gave out and she had to stay in bed for three days straight.

To make matters worse, now that they were back home, she began to really notice the class and cultural differences between herself and her husband. She felt like a contemporary Eliza Doolittle. "That whole 'jungle girl' thing started to get really ugly," she once told me. "It was like he polished me up, taught me things, and showed me off to his screenwriter friends."

Maricela thought about leaving Jason, but reasoned that she deserved the abuse because of all that she had put him through. In June 2003, *he* gave *her* an ultimatum: "If you don't get better by our anniversary in March 2004, I will leave you." On Valentine's Day 2004, he officially asked for a separation. Maricela finally left and moved back in with her family.

In past years, it was commonly accepted that about 30 percent of veterans suffer from PTSD at some point, but recent controversy over diagnosis has put that number into question.

Even Columbia University's Robert L. Spitzer and Michael B. First, who supervised the last two editions of the *Diagnostic and Statistical Manual of Mental Disorders*—the most widely regarded manual for psychologists—believe that PTSD is vastly overdiagnosed. The danger of such a vague catchall diagnosis is that vets may not be getting the specific kind of care they need— an anxiety disorder, for example, is treated far differently from clinical depression. And further, the Department of Veterans Affairs' current approach to PTSD may not encourage recovery. As investigative reporter David Dobbs writes in a 2009 *Scientific American* article, "Unlike a vet who has lost a leg, a vet with PTSD loses disability benefits as soon as he recovers or starts working. The entire system seems designed to encourage chronic disability."

The benefits of a PTSD framework, however, are alive and well in this exchange between Maricela and Raul. It names something they've felt, legitimizes their suffering. And unlike "depression"—which is a difficult term to own within the culture they share—PTSD has a more official ring. It seems like something that happened to you, rather than something that developed from within you. For some, it feels like a safer pain to claim.

"It's a real thing," Maricela reassures Raul. "How did you heal?"

"I don't know," Raul says, shrugging. "I guess just time. And the work. I got back into the work with the youth." Raul has still never been to therapy.

"Yeah, that's what's healing me too," Maricela says. "And therapy." Eventually Maricela got professional help, even though her family was unfamiliar and uncomfortable with it. She found art therapy the most healing. "I called that therapist Mary Poppins, because she always had this big bag that she would pull art supplies out of," she says, smiling. "At first I thought it might be hokey to sit there drawing, but it actually did allow me to open up." She also got into knitting.

It's interesting to watch Maricela and Raul interact, I realize, for another reason. Each lives in a very gender-segregated world. Maricela has found solace in women. She of course interacts with men on a daily basis, but her true confidants these days are her female roommate (a therapist specializing in veterans' issues); her mentor, Eli Painted Crow; and the SWAN cofounders—all women. Raul lives in a world of men. His clients are mostly male. The two caseworkers he supervises are men. He battles social ills marinated in machismo all day long. Further, the Mexican culture that they share seems, not uniquely but certainly intensely, gender-segregated—the men often gone, the women caretaking, cooking, scraping by. There is a palpable tenderness between Maricela and Raul as they speak about their common struggles, almost a junior high nervousness.

Raul's cell phone incessantly beeps and vibrates on the tabletop, and eventually he lets it lure him away. "It was great to meet you, Maricela. Just let me know. I can hook you up. Just call."

"I will, thank you so much," Maricela says, standing up to shake his hand.

JUNE 2004. MARICELA WALKED into the bedroom of her childhood home, opened the bottle of sleeping pills on her bureau, and poured about fifty pills onto the bed. Then she started slugging them down, a handful at a time. "It was as if it happened instantly," she says. In fact, her desperation had been developing over time; she had been fighting with her siblings and having nasty, toxic conversations with her ex-husband, who was characterizing her as a "gold digger," and she had found that leaving him had done nothing to stave off her PTSD symptoms. She still hadn't told a soul about her rape.

Maricela's heavy eyelids ached open as her mother's panicked face hovered over her, tears streaming down her face. She screamed over and over: "*Velas, mi hija! Velas!*" (Stay awake, my daughter! Stay awake!)

When Maricela tells me about this moment, she tears up for the first time in our many conversations. "I thought I was taking my last breath," she says. "I had survived up to that point by telling stories—about the corrupt military, about my abusive husband, about screwed-up American politics. I was telling the truth, just not the whole truth." The whole truth would emerge only when Maricela found a group of other women veterans that gave her permission to speak it.

MARICELA'S CHURCH BECAME the Santa Monica pier. Starting in 2004, she would go every Sunday, right around 7:30 a.m., and slip into the quiet line of people that snaked underneath the pier toward stacks of white crosses—one for each American casualty in the Iraq War. She loved the feeling of the heavy wood in her hands, the physical exertion of trudging up the beach to place the cross, and then the smell of the early morning ocean as she headed back to the pier to get another. It was physical, visceral, communal.

She first discovered this ritual through an empathic English professor at Santa Monica College, where she decided to finish up her degree after leaving the military. He was part of the Los Angeles chapter of Veterans for Peace, which hosted this weekly reminder of the cost of war—calling it "Arlington West." At dawn, they would place the crosses in the cool beach sand, and at dusk, they would remove them and restack them under the pier.

"It was very therapeutic for me," Maricela says. "At first I kept to myself—just showed up each Sunday and worked alongside the other volunteers, had my moment, and then left. But then I started to get to know some of the other people." By August 2005

Maricela was a fixture in the community and was invited down to Crawford, Texas, to camp out near President George W. Bush's ranch with other veterans against the war.

A tight-knit group of about a hundred veterans, many of them women, sat around in the dead heat and swapped stories of their time in Iraq and its often painful aftermath. Maricela learned about PTSD for the first time. She didn't yet recognize her own symptoms, believing that only those who had "seen combat" could have PTSD. (This is a major misconception held by a lot of veterans, especially women, who don't realize that violent experiences outside of official combat are all too common and often similarly triggering.)

That experience led to many others, including an all-female retreat in Los Angeles in 2006—hosted by a peer support organization called Vets 4 Vets—where for the first time Maricela heard women veterans speak about being raped in the military. As one woman bravely described her attack and the years of shame and silence that followed, Maricela sat still as a statue, stunned. Every word, every feeling expressed, was familiar. It was as if she were being awakened from the dead.

Just hours later, Maricela sat down with the two therapists who were on site, both women, and said, "I think I need to talk."

"Okay," said one, gently moving forward. "The first thing we ask all of our women veterans is: have you ever been sexually assaulted?"

Maricela sobbed, her silence finally broken.

SHORTLY AFTER, MARICELA FINALLY got into steady therapy and started to get more and more involved in the antiwar movement. She also went down to New Orleans for two weeks to "run away" and help out. Maricela loved the work. Being down in the Lower Ninth Ward reconnected her to some of her early memories of the L.A. riots: "I saw my city burned too." Helping out with the rebuilding effort felt healing in a very personal way. She was finally able to sleep through the night.

She loved it so much that a few months later, she planned and facilitated a trip down to New Orleans for Vets 4 Vets. The twenty veterans that accompanied her were able to come together and find some respite from their racing minds through the all-consuming, physical work of reconstruction (gutting houses, putting up drywall). Maricela was proud of her efforts, pitching to Vets 4 Vets that she would also like to organize a writing retreat for a group of female veterans. The executive director at the time was lukewarm on the idea, but said that if Maricela would organize another general retreat first, he would fund her all-female retreat.

As Maricela continued to get involved in antiwar activism, she started to notice that some of the same racist and sexist dynamics of the U.S. military were being played out on a smaller stage, to a lesser scale, among antimilitary leaders. At the Veterans for Peace convention in 2006, she noticed that the majority of those who were chosen as spokespeople were white and male. She also continued to hear "combat" emphasized, as if those who hadn't seen a roadside bomb explode couldn't really know suffering or hadn't really earned their right to speak out against the war on the national stage. (It's ironic to hear that the antiwar movement is romanticizing war in its effort to denounce it.)

Maricela kept these observations mostly to herself, not wanting to "rock the boat," until she met Eli Painted Crow, who would become her lifelong friend and mentor. Maricela says, "When I first met Eli, I was intimidated. She was so strong. She really validated all of these things I'd seen but didn't want to say anything about because I thought I should just do what was good for the cause. Eli pointed out that there was a real lack of diversity among the antiwar leadership. For the first time I realized it wasn't just something wrong with me. It was something wrong with the movement."

It dawned on Maricela that she had been doing unpaid labor for Vets 4 Vets without even considering that she might deserve compensation, much less asking whether her peer organizers— mostly men—were being paid. When she tried to initiate these conversations with the leadership at Vets 4 Vets, she was rebuffed, even guilt-tripped. They insinuated that any time or money not spent on direct services meant risking further suicides among veterans. For a woman who had once given up on life herself, this was the final, manipulative straw.

She wanted a group of her own.

EVERY ONCE IN A WHILE, a smile breaks the surface of Maricela's face, and it's as if I catch a glimpse of her spirit intact—before she was betrayed by the military, by that man in the stairwell, by the false promise of happily ever after. The first time it happens is when I ask her about her work at McDonald's.

"I would study people there," she says, and then fondly remembers one of her favorite customers—an old black man who grumbled his way in each morning around the same time and ordered a courtesy cup with ice, a coffee with two Equals and two creams, and a biscuit with strawberry jelly. One day Maricela decided to prepare his breakfast for him ahead of time, lovingly setting each item on a tray. When he arrived, she simply slid it across the Formica counter triumphantly.

"His behavior instantly switched," she says, her smile lit up, her eyes wide and bright. "He went from Oscar the Grouch to Big Bird, all because he felt that people noticed him, that he belonged."

The last time I see Maricela truly light up is in the parking lot of Homeboy Industries. "What's your favorite color?" she asks abruptly as we're parting ways.

"I've always been torn between blue and green," I answer. "Why?"

"One of the things I do to deal with the PTSD is knit."

"Awesome," I reply, touched.

"It's really calming. I'll knit you a scarf. I'll even give you the special pattern that only SWAN members have," she says, that rare and luminous smile spreading across her face. It is the smile of a little girl taking delicious pleasure in inviting a new friend into the clubhouse. It is the smile of hard-earned, and still too fleeting, happiness.

The Boxer
Emily Abt, filmmaker, New York City

"I was a bona fide wannabe," Emily Abt says, laughing and shaking her head as she tears off a piece of her panino. "I tweezed my eyebrows really thin, got a poodle perm, wore super-baggy clothes. People used to ask if I was Puerto Rican because I fronted so hard."

It's hard to believe, looking at thirty-four-year-old, unmistakably white Emily in her skinny jeans, red and white zip-up sweater, and pink scarf. She grew up in Cambridge, Massachusetts, and went to Concord Academy, one of the most prestigious private high schools in the country. Her mother is an expert in microlending to African countries, and her father, a refugee from Nazi Germany, is the founder of a well-regarded consulting firm called Abt Associates. Emily is petite, beautiful, blonde. In fact, there are only two traces of her adolescence left behind: her bright red leather high-top Reeboks and the way the language of hip-hop culture drips off her tongue effortlessly.

"I remember going to Black Student Organization dances and having a sore ass the next day from trying to stick it out all night," Emily adds, still laughing. After a short pause, she looks up, shrugs her shoulders, and says, "I wanted hip-hop, but it didn't want me."

EMILY ABT HAS COME a long way. Today she is an award-winning filmmaker right on the brink of a certain sort of recognition that few women ever get in such a male-dominated industry. She has her own production company, Pureland Pictures. She's single-handedly raised over one million dollars for her films—most of it from women. She's made two acclaimed documentaries: *Take It From Me*, on welfare reform, and *All of Us*, on HIV/AIDS infection among African American women. Her documentary work has been lauded in publications from the *New York Times* to *People* magazine and has been screened on PBS, on Showtime, and at colleges and conferences throughout the nation.

Emily's first full-length narrative film, *Toe to Toe*, debuted in 2009 "in competition" at Sundance—the most prestigious category. It is a brutal look at adolescent female friendship, made even more complex by the trinity of race, class, and sexuality. It was distributed domestically by Strand and abroad by Regent Releasing—two well-respected independent film distributors—in 2010. She also was courted by talent agencies and got lots of exposure; *Daily Variety* even named her one of "Ten Directors to Watch."

Emily explains, "For any independent American filmmaker, Sundance is the holy grail. You toil around in obscurity for years, and then the second you get into Sundance, they all show up and compete for you. I'm not going to pretend it isn't fun."

ACCEPTANCE IS NOT SOMETHING that Emily has come by easily. Her high school days were filled with failed attempts at a distinct identity. Unlike her mostly wealthy peers at Concord Academy who sought to fit in, Emily always wanted to stand out. She memorized rap songs instead of SAT vocabulary, wore Adidas instead of flip-flops, and lusted after the scholarship kids instead of the Dave Matthews Band–obsessed skier boys.

A mediocre student compared to her superdiligent peers, Emily was drawn to filmmaking, but one of her favorite teachers told her, "Don't go to film school. You don't have any good stories to tell yet." She heeded his advice and decided on New York University (NYU). Emily dreamed of finally fitting in with the hip-hop scene in the city where it all started.

She did everything right. Got the *Vibe* magazine internship. Started hanging out at the right clubs, going to the right shows, even dating legendary break-dancer Crazy Legs (nine years her senior). But there was always that discomfiting feeling in the pit of her stomach that she wasn't, nor would she ever be, truly accepted. She knew the guys at the *Vibe* office saw her as just another white girl trying to be down; interestingly, they embraced the Jewish girl with dark hair who managed to pass for Chicana. Emily says, "It was weird to meet white girls who were more confused than I was."

She also met girls who were actually from the neighborhoods—Bed-Stuy, the Bronx, Harlem—that she'd memorized so many rap lyrics about, and it was as if they saw right through her. Maria, a Spanish girl who grew up in New York City, became one of her best friends. "Maria checked me hard," Emily says. "She grew up in this really patriarchal family, so she was all about feminism." At Emily's wedding, Maria told the story of their first encounter: "This girl walked in from the 'hard streets' of Cambridge with big hoop earrings and red Cross Colours jeans. I was like, 'Who is this Barbie doll pretending to be?'"

Looking back, Emily doesn't know what motivated her to adopt the aesthetics of hip-hop and ache to be part of the culture so hungrily. "I've thought about it so much, and I'm still not really sure why I wanted to be part of it all so bad," she says.

But before long, our conversation drifts to the romance of suffering, and I hear a connection loud and clear. Emily says, "I've always been attracted to stories of pain. Maybe it's my father's connection to the Holocaust or just growing up in such a privileged environment, but I've always sought out people who've been through hard times."

Eventually Emily left the world of hip-hop and followed Maria into the NYU Women's Center. It was there that she discovered a feminist critique of hip-hop. "There was just so much internalized misogyny in the lyrics I was listening to on a regular basis," Emily says. Her mind was blown by bell hooks, the author of books like *Feminism Is for Everybody* and *Killing Rage*. She read Naomi Wolf's *The Beauty Myth* and realized she'd been walking around in baggy clothes for the last ten years because, in part, she was ashamed of her skinniness. She bought some new clothes and unveiled her "cute figure"—as Maria put it—to the world. She took a feminist writing class and reclaimed her own voice; she got glowing feedback from the professor and started to come into her intellectual own. "I had been sleepwalking through high school," she laments. "But walking into that Women's Center finally woke me up."

Emily was still obsessed with issues of race and class, but she was learning how to process them through her own hardearned perspective (influenced by hip-hop, feminism, and her achievement-oriented, tough-love family). "I felt left out for so long," she says, "like I was fighting to get in. Finally, I just said 'fuck it' and found myself."

I nod, recognizing a lot of myself in Emily's story of adolescent struggle. I was never bold enough to fully try on an alternate identity; the leap from middle-class Colorado Springs suburbia to true-blue hip-hop head always seemed impossibly large. But I did—like so many white kids in the nineties—become enraptured by hip-hop's seductive beats and raw lyrics. Common and Mos Def and OutKast, even the harsher lyrics of Tupac and Nas, spoke with a beauty and an honesty that was mostly absent from the suburban culture that I was rebelling against—polite, politically correct, safe. I too moved to New York City in search of something grittier, something more "real." And I too found myself at home in feminism, forced to confront questions of authenticity and my own attraction to suffering.

In fact, it's a common coming-of-age tale of so many privileged white girls with a passion for words and a propensity for altruism in contemporary America. We've struggled to understand our own relationship to struggle. We've often failed miserably. And, best-case scenario, we're wiser because of it.

Why this penchant for getting up close to others' pain? Why the deliberate seeking for stories of violence and despair? Because we have a basic hunger for meaning that will not be satiated by homecoming or the honor roll. For many, meaning is derived from persevering, resisting, fighting. It is born out of big struggles, not petty dramas. In *War Is a Force That Gives Us Meaning*, Chris Hedges writes, "We are tempted to reduce life to a simple search for happiness. Happiness, however, withers if there is no meaning."

Girls like Emily and me, unpracticed in the subtleties of struggle, overlook the pain hidden in the lives of our own families and neighborhoods. (To our credit, white folks tend to be masterful at this particular brand of obfuscation.) It wasn't until graduate school, for example, that I finally faced my own family's history of mental illness. It wasn't until *Toe to Toe* that Emily explored deprivation and desperation of a white, privileged variety.

Emily is grateful for her coming-of-age, characterized by so many rejections and reinventions. The struggle to explore her own relationship to struggle became its own source of meaning. "I was really just trying to be something that I wasn't. In retrospect, I realize that it was a beautiful thing that the hip-hop world never let me in, because it has informed so much of my work. I keep it ridiculously real now."

I VISIT THE OFFICE of Pureland, Emily's production company, on a Wednesday afternoon. It's deep in warehouse land of Brooklyn, near the Gowanus Canal. The big silver industrial door on the building has DAYDREAM written across it in red fading paint. It's not a word I associate with Emily—she's all tough love and business. "I'm a warrior for my films," she once told me.

Pureland's cozy space, which the staff has inhabited for two years, is impeccably organized. There are big metal shelves right when you enter, each one labeled: COMPOSER SAMPLES, DVDs AND CLIENT MASTERS, REELS. There's a copy of *Do the Right Thing* and an *MLA Handbook,* mammoth three-ring binders filled with production notes, and Fela Kuti and Portishead CDs.

Off to the right is an impeccably clean bathroom and a small editing room with two huge monitors, a six-by-six-foot storyboard covered in fluorescent index cards, and a framed poster of the most famous image that came out of the Tiananmen Square protests in 1989: a solitary man standing resolutely in front of four giant tanks.

Inside the main room of the office—all modern, clean lines— four people buzz around: trying to fix a broken Mac computer, getting mailings ready for film festival entry (a whiteboard lists all of those that are coming up, along with their deadlines), sitting at a computer with massive headphones, talking on the phone. Emily briefly introduces me to everyone, and they politely wave or smile before going back to their work. They are all young people of color, three women and one guy.

Sunshine floods in from a couple of giant windows and illuminates Emily's space, which is sectioned off from the rest of the room with a divider. "Sorry about my outfit," Emily says. "I've got a meeting with the William Morris people." William Morris has signed on to be Emily's agency—representing her in L.A., setting up meetings for her with producers, and getting her speaking gigs at colleges and conferences. Emily is dressed in wide-legged wool pants and a fitted sweater. She's spent the morning putting together some ideas for the prestigious agency on what she might speak about: "Picasso Was a Businessman Too: Making Art and Making a Living" and "Race Relations on the Film Set," among others.

Emily is scheduled to do a series of what are called "general meetings" in L.A. with some big-time producers. They've all seen and liked *Toe to Toe*, and the goal is to create relationships with people who might feed her screenwriting or directing jobs down the line or be interested in producing her next project—no small feat in one of the last bona fide boys' clubs existing in America.

She's beyond ready. Her husband, a philosopher of science, has just been hired to teach at Princeton. Emily was also offered a position teaching film. Both of their families are overjoyed and so is Emily, but she's worried that her own career could get lost in the shuffle. She'd been hoping he might get hired at a university in Los Angeles, an organic move for her career, but now it looks like that won't be possible. "I'm taking one for the team here," Emily tells me.

She's well beyond her scrappy twenties, ready to make money, ready for life to be a little bit easier, ready to fight a little less hard. Having successful meetings in L.A. could make that happen. It could prove—to herself, to her family, to the industry—that she's official.

"We're trying to relaunch our advertising business, fix a computer, and submit to all these festivals," Emily says, "so we're a little crazy around here." Pureland shoots corporate campaigns, public service announcements, commercials, and anything else they can get to try to keep the company afloat. "Gotta rob Peter to pay Paul," Emily says wistfully as she organizes the printouts for William Morris.

Emily made a grand total of $14,000 last year, just $4,000 above the poverty line for a single woman. It's something she brings up frequently in our conversations, citing the fact that she is now thirty-four years old, married, looking to have babies. "I'm a grown-ass woman. I can't keep living like this."

But her financial situation is more complicated than that. While her income has consistently been far below that of her college-educated peers, she also has a few critical sources of stability that most young people in her tax bracket wouldn't dream of—starting with a home. Her aunt, a feminist philanthropist and artist, bought Emily an apartment in Brooklyn's Park Slope neighborhood in the spirit of providing "a room of one's own," à la Virginia Woolf. Emily is incredibly grateful for the gift and recognizes that it is probably the one thing that has kept her from giving up on her filmmaking dreams: "It has been my lifeboat. Seriously."

Emily has also had access to funding sources in a way that aspiring filmmakers from less privileged backgrounds simply don't. Much of the forty thousand dollars it took to make her first documentary, *Take It from Me*, was subsidized by friends and family. She's received over fifteen grants for her work (including a Fulbright), but has still had to return to her network for donations in order to make *All of Us*, which cost $300,000 in total. For *Toe to Toe*, her feature debut, she had to go back to her community once again. It cost a total of $750,000. "It gets to a point when it's just humiliating to keep asking your inner circle for money," Emily says. "You wonder if they're thinking, 'Shouldn't her art be paying for itself by now?'"

Emily has waitressed, made promotional videos for corporations, shot Bar Mitzvahs and reality television—you name it, she's done it. Her aunt gave her a copy of a book called *Women Don't Ask*, by Linda Babcock and Sara Laschever, and ever since she's been fearless about fund-raising: "It's all a numbers game. If you don't want it enough to be uncomfortable and ask for the funding, then you shouldn't be making the film. That might sound harsh, but I think that film schools do aspiring filmmakers a disservice by acting like this isn't going to be a huge part of getting started in the business."

Emily went to the film program at Columbia University, one of the best in the country, for her master's in fine arts and remembers that one of the strongest filmmakers in her class, a single mom, had to drop out halfway through because of the financial constraints. "I hated seeing her go," she says. "She had so much amazing work in her."

Beyond the class constraints, of course, is the gender discrimination. In 2008 only 9 percent of all directors working on the top 250 films were women. In Emily's other roles, she is also a minority—only 12 percent of top-grossing films were written by women and only 16 percent were executive produced by them. Dr. Martha M. Lauzen, executive director of the Center for the Study of Women in Television and Film, who compiles these statistics annually, calls this the "celluloid ceiling."

I spot a collection of tiny Buddha figurines on a small shelf in the corner of the office. "What's that all about?" I ask, pointing. Emily laughs and says, "'Pureland' actually means 'Buddhist heaven.' It's sort of ironic, because of course I am, like, the total opposite of the Buddha. Ask these guys," she says, motioning to the crew behind her. One woman with a head wrap and huge brown eyes raises one eyebrow and smiles mischievously. "I aspire to it," Emily adds. "I do, but it's just not in my nature or the nature of this business. It's a constant hustle."

EMILY DIDN'T GO DIRECTLY into filmmaking. In fact, her first job out of NYU was a whole different kind of hustle. She was a caseworker with WEP (Work Eligibility Program), a government program designed to get welfare recipients into jobs. Every day she commuted from her apartment in Brooklyn to a cramped office deluged in paperwork right next to Port Authority—"the armpit of New York," as she describes it. "The worst was the resident crackhead who hung out outside. On a good day she'd wear pants. On a bad day she'd just go without."

Emily's coworkers were mostly middle-aged black and Latina women, many of them possessing that paradoxical mix of endless empathy and short tempers. "They taught me not to be a sucka," Emily says. "So many of my clients were amazing—salt-of-the-earth people who had just gotten screwed. I really wanted to help them. But other clients were shady." She pauses, looking up as if she's imagining a client in particular. "I mean, it makes sense. People have to scheme as a means of survival. But sometimes it turns into laziness, and then you have to give them tough love."

Emily couldn't get over the feeling that she wasn't in the right place (again). She didn't feel good at her job. She certainly didn't enjoy it. "I was downright miserable," she says. "But I had this idea that doing social work was going to get me into the pearly gates." She also felt stuck because she'd conceived of a five-year plan for her life: do social work for a few years, get into a top ten law school, become a public servant.

Meanwhile, kids she had grown up with were experimenting with careers in creative fields, working at plush dot-com jobs with pool tables and happy hours, and generally appearing way less burned out than Emily felt. She was jealous, but tried to dismiss her envy as frivolous; this denial only hardened her sense of martyrdom.

Emily was broken open one night while speaking to one of her older brother's friends—a guy she'd always looked up to who taught in the New York City public school system. After hearing Emily talk about how miserable she was at her job, he told her, "You're not doing anyone any favors if you don't follow your dreams. Hell, you're probably not even doing a very good job if you're that miserable."

Emily knew he was right. She realized that she had been "getting her rocks off on being morally superior," but wasn't actually inspired by the work. She had never lost her high school dream of making movies. When Emily found out that she didn't get into law school, she felt as if her fate was sealed. She quit her job and started following a few of her most interesting former clients around with a cheap camera. Looking back, she realizes: "I fought harder to tell the story of a welfare recipient than I ever fought for one as a caseworker.

"That's when I revealed myself as a false altruist," she admits. "I was doing what I thought I was supposed to be doing, but I wasn't effective. I'm not going to wrap myself in a flag and say the world needs my films, but I do think I've managed to change a few lives. I'm not sure I could say the same of my social work."

Emily's painful journey reminds me of educator Parker Palmer's apt wisdom: "Each of us arrives here with a nature, which means both limits and potentials. We can learn as much about our nature by running into our limits as by experiencing our potential."

EMILY BELIEVES THAT HER EXPERIENCES as a caseworker ended up being perfect training for making documentary films about social issues, because she knew how to set boundaries. The film-making process is so intimate that filmmakers inevitably create relationships with their subjects; this closeness, in fact, is imperative to an honest, engaging film. But that also means that filmmakers are forced into the almost unbearable position of witnessing the suffering—physical, financial, emotional, spiritual—of their subjects and doing nothing. When you add the class and cultural dynamics present in films like Emily's—where the director and the folks she's following come from two totally different worlds—you've got all kinds of moral complexity.

"Some filmmakers get destroyed by their own empathy," Emily says. "I've heard of a filmmaker who adopted one of her subject's kids. I know others who have given their subjects all kinds of money, and it's not like these are artists with a whole lot of money to begin with."

She says, "I only got played once." A daughter of one of her subjects called her up in desperation, saying that the cupboards were bare and there was nothing for the many children in the house to eat. "I rode the train all the way up to the Bronx on a Sunday afternoon with arms full of groceries," Emily says. "When I got there and started putting them away, I realized that there was plenty of food in the house. I vowed to myself that I would never get played again."

There have been times when her resistance to interfere has appeared downright cruel. While shooting *Take It from Me*, her documentary about the welfare system, she once held the camera on a wailing baby being torn from the arms of his mother and handed over to foster care. "I knew people were looking at me like I was a monster," Emily says. "But I also knew that this was the shot that was going to literally make the film. Ultimately, making the most impact on people who might see the film someday was more important than anything I could have done in that moment."

Emily believes that the most ethical thing she can do is to be as transparent with her subjects as they are with her. "If they're going to open up their lives to me, I sure as hell better keep it real with them," she says. "If I'm coming into their space, then they have every right to know about my privileged little white-girl world too. I'm like, 'Hey, I grew up with a pool.' Frontin' like I'm anything other than what I am would be disingenuous." Hard-earned wisdom, of course.

While Emily tries not to interfere with her subjects' lives, she will tell them the truth about what she thinks. For example, one of her subjects would swat at her small children and curse at them when she lost her temper. Emily told her, "Don't treat them that way in front of me. I think it's abusive."

It's all part of Emily's theory of social courage—the missing ingredient of racial progress in this country. She says, "White people have to stop apologizing. I think America is ready for that, but we have to stop pretending that we're something we're not or tiptoeing around one another. It keeps us from creating real relationships."

Emily never tiptoes. It's part of her personality, and it's reflected in the intensity of her films. *All of Us,* her documentary on HIV/AIDS infection rates among women, is a painful film to watch and was even more painful to make. One of the main characters, Tara, was raped at five years old, survived years of drug addiction and prostitution but contracted HIV, and had to have invasive surgery for cervical cancer. Tara revealed that she didn't have the courage to tell her boyfriend that she was in too much pain to have sex. She eventually passed away; the viewer is left with profound sadness over watching a woman die before she's learned to stick up for herself.

Emily also followed a young doctor, Mehret Mandefro, in *All of Us.* During the course of the film, Mehret is trying to study why the infection rate is so high among African American women. She applies for a long-shot grant, travels to her home country, Ethiopia, and creates important friendships with many HIV-infected women in the South Bronx, where she works.

But instead of letting Mehret, one of Emily's closest friends at the time, be comfortably cast as the do-gooder doctor, Emily pushes her to talk about her own sex life. Mehret admits to having unprotected sex with a guy she's falling for, creating a really important moment in the film when doctor and patient are revealed to be equally fallible and beautifully human. Mehret also hosts a little party at her apartment, where a diverse group of girlfriends, Emily included, share openly about their experiences with sex and protection, self-love and a lack thereof.

But even the other women's transparency could not stave off Mehret's negative reaction when she saw the completed film. After months of painful and protracted conflict, sometimes involving lawyers, Mehret finally gave up on convincing Emily to change the cut, but their close friendship dissolved. It was a tumultuous and heartbreaking time for Emily.

"I almost let that one go," she reflects. It was hard to defend her vision for the film—one in which educated and uneducated women were equalized, one in which women were brutally honest about the risks they take with their own sexual health, one free of saints. Mehret was upset, and even Emily's longtime editor recommended pulling the incriminating footage. But Emily stood firm. "It was my baby," she says. Emily frequently refers to her films as if they were her own children. "I knew that it wouldn't be half as powerful if we glossed over what Mehret was going through."

I ask, "Do you ever feel conflicted about telling these women's stories? I mean, that's a lot of responsibility."

She looks at me knowingly and says, "You know what? The only people who bring that up are other privileged white people. There aren't enough people telling these kinds of stories."

EMILY IS SCREENING *All of Us* at Bronx Community College on a Tuesday afternoon. There are about forty people in the room, sitting on metal folding chairs, most of them students. The only two white women in the room are both professors. Big windows line one wall, but they have been covered with a haphazard combination of curtains and tablecloths to block out the light.

A young Latina woman with a wool hat, arms covered in tattoos, and dangly earrings in the shape of wings asks Emily, "It seems like this film would be really emotionally draining to make. How did you keep going?"

Emily smiles and replies, "I'll be honest with you. It was draining. I'd be sitting in the doctor's office with Tara and, you know, filming, but my hand was just shaking. It was so awful to have to watch her in so much pain and hear that she would be facing even more of it. The thing that kept us going were the statistics. We were sure we would get scooped. Scooped is a journalist term for when someone else tells the story that you're working on before you get a chance to. But sadly, we didn't. There just aren't enough people talking about this issue."

Many in the crowd nod their heads, churchlike, and then Emily asks, "Any more questions?" After a few seconds she says, "Well, thanks so much for coming out. I've got copies of the film for sale if anyone is interested, and if you want to set up a screening in your community or anything, please be in touch. I just really appreciate the opportunity." Emily is very intimate with audiences; each one of her responses communicates that she is "just like you" and also very grateful. Far from a diva who just got back from Sundance, she exudes a "power to the people" vibe—like she'd be happy to screen her film in your living room, as long as it meant that people would be informed and inspired by it.

Everyone applauds and begins to wander out. A few guys linger to ask Emily questions about how she "made it" in filmmaking. One of them, a heavyset guy in a Kangol hat with square-rimmed black glasses, identifies himself as the head of the film society at the college. "My friends and I are putting together all of our money to make a feature in May," he tells Emily. "The goal is to do four features by next fall. We'll see what happens."

"Stick with it!" Emily says, "It sounds like you've got the bug." She's encouraging to everyone, passing out business cards, giving the aspiring filmmakers free DVDs and book recommendations.

After Emily takes some pictures with the crew of guys and some professors, we wander out to the parking lot and get into her car. She's heading straight from the screening to the Lower East Side, where she's scheduled an interview with a young politician. Emily's newest screenplay, still in the research phase, is about a biracial female politician who has to wrestle with identity issues while running for office. As Emily plugs an address into her GPS system, she reflects on how a group of girls started crying during the screening of *All of Us*: "That dark-skinned sister in the back was literally sobbing. It's hard, you know; you invoke emotions like that, and you just hope it is cathartic for people."

One of the weeping girls raised her hand during the Q&A and

told Emily, "My mom doesn't have HIV, but she went through a lot of this stuff. I wish she could see this film." Then she asked, "How did it change you to make the film?"

Emily told her, "This film totally changed my life. During the 'truth circle' I realized that I wasn't always a hundred percent careful either." Now, back in the car, Emily shakes her head and says, "There but for the grace of God go I. It could have been me."

"Well, yes and no," I respond. "I mean, Tara and Chevelle [the other HIV-positive character in Emily's film] grew up in very different circumstances. You never had to resort to prostitution. Chances are you never had sex with an intravenous drug user. There are systemic influences that set these women up, you know? It wasn't just about choices."

"That's what Mehret always said—that I didn't have enough of a critique of institutional racism," Emily answers. "But the way I see it, do we want to teach women how to complain more about the system? Or do we want to tell them, 'Take your life into your own hands; only you can save yourself'?"

This struggle—between the system and the self, long-term and short-term change, the political and the personal—is one of the most palpable tensions that I see, not just in Emily's films, but in all social justice work. The most effective activists that I encounter are those who can hold both levels in their overworked minds and their overwhelmed hearts at once. They study the unique texture of bark on a single tree while still seeing the entire landscape of forest.

This doesn't mean that to be an effective activist one must deal on both levels all of the time. Raul, for example, isn't interested in—nor does he have time for—focusing on prison reform. He's sitting in the stuffy visiting room, looking into the eyes of a teenage boy, advocating for his unique needs in court. But Raul's work is also greatly improved by his capacity to communicate his experiences with the Homebody Industries team so that they might affect policy.

It seems far easier to manifest a dual approach—alleviating the suffering of individuals while changing the system that created their suffering in the first place—when one is part of an organization. Emily is just one artist, with one chance to shape a beautiful, affecting film. Seeing her audience as the individual women she wants to reach, rather than the system that shapes them, makes a lot of sense.

She says, "I make my films for those girls crying in that room." She's driving along the street now. We're surrounded by the sights, smells, and sounds of the Bronx wafting in through the cracked windows. I struggle to take notes as Emily deftly changes lanes, her stick-shift transmission purring, and we turn onto the FDR.

A DENTAL APPOINTMENT is not generally thought of as the first stop on the way to Hollywood. Nonetheless, one of Emily's most serendipitous moments on her journey toward filmmaking took place during a standard cleaning in 1999 on the Upper West Side.

As she got up to leave, the dentist noticed a copy of *Story* by Robert McKee peeking out of her bag. "Are you an aspiring screenwriter?" he asked, stripping off his latex gloves with a thwack.

"I'd like to do it all," Emily answered. "Write, direct, produce."

"Well, then, you'll have to meet my daughter," he said, scribbling her name and number on a pharmaceutical memo pad. "She's a producer. I'm sure she'd be willing to sit down with you for a cup of coffee, at the very least."

"Wow, thank you so much," Emily said, looking down at the note and reading PAMELA KOFFLER. As if the idea of getting filmmaker connections through your dentist wasn't preposterous enough, Emily had just been given access to the executive producer of the soon-to-be indy hit of Hollywood, *Boys Don't Cry*.

Emily did far more than get a coffee with Koffler. She ended up interning for her (long, exhausting hours for no money) and eventually being invited to work on the set of *Boys Don't Cry* in Dallas, Texas. She did everything and anything—coordinated extras on set, drove the electricians (who made a sport out of teasing her) around, ran errands for the hard-ass assistant director who wouldn't let anyone sit down on set.

"Even though I was literally working eighteen-hour days," Emily says, "I was totally alive during that time. I was watching Kim [Kimberly Pierce, writer/director] on set and thinking, 'I *want* that job!'"

Emily had read the script before production: "I believed in that film. I had a feeling that it was going to be really good." Indeed, it would go on to win forty-two awards, including an Oscar. Nobody benefited from the film's success more than Hilary Swank, whose career was launched by her brave portrayal of transgender teenager Brandon Teena. But Emily Abt was launched, too, in a less public way. She truly understood, for the first time, what it was going to take to survive as a woman writer/director, and even though it looked hellish—being challenged on set, called a bitch, forced to stand up for your vision constantly—it was what she wanted more than anything else.

Emily loved making social-issue documentaries, but she also recognized that the market would always be limited. "I had to make a more commercial film if I wanted to expand my audience and make a name for myself," Emily says. "After seeing Kimberly at work, I realized that I could do that while also tackling some of the issues that are most important to me."

EMILY LEARNED HOW TO WRITE screenplays while in film school at Columbia, and also by working and reworking *Toe to Toe*. It is the story of two teenage girls—one black, one white—who both attend a college-prep school in the D.C. area. Tosha, the black girl, is on scholarship and struggling with her dual roles as both the only hope of her family and the sellout of her neighborhood. Jesse, the white girl, is sexually promiscuous as a way to seek attention that she's not getting from her career-obsessed single mother. They are both flawed and both courageous in their own ways.

Not surprisingly, Emily's inspiration for the film was an antagonistic friendship of her own in high school. I spot pieces of Emily in both Tosha and Jesse—Tosha is painstakingly organized, and Jesse has a mother who does international development work. They're both fish-out-of-water figures, but not surprisingly, Jesse is far less comfortable in her own skin. She moves through the world of the film as if perpetually hungry. Emily made sure that she was often shot from above—turning her into a lost little girl in a big, modern house.

But Tosha has her own demons to battle. "I refuse to make a black Jesus figure, like so many white filmmakers these days. I don't kiss their asses," Emily attests. She's referring to big Hollywood movies like *The Green Mile* and *The Curious Case of Benjamin Button*, in which the black characters are solely endearing and virtuous. "To deny the complexity of black folks is racist," she adds.

Emily recruited some of her main actors from a TV show with a cult following: *The Wire*. In fact, Emily says that if she aspires to emulate anyone's work, it is that of David Simon—the controversial creator of the show and longtime newspaper journalist. "I want to write great characters that are public servants, like Simon does, and pay homage to them," Emily says. "They're better people than me. They deserve the spotlight."

Simon, a white guy from D.C., is known for his fearless portraits of inner city life, a world he got to know well as a crime reporter for the *Baltimore Sun*. Anger—at former bosses, at screwed-up bureaucracies, at hypocrisy—has often been his artistic motivation. An *Atlantic* profile on him was headlined "The Angriest Man in Television."

There's an important difference between Emily's worldview and Simon's. While Emily's Jesse is designed to make teenage girls think twice about using sex to get attention, and Tosha is a warning about the dangers of blind striving, the only one of Simon's "characters" that is supposed to inspire self-reflection is the system itself—bureaucratic, dysfunctional, heartless, broken. His characters—drug dealers, police officers, and politicians alike—are all corrupt on some level, but they're not meant to be symbols of anything other than the amoral nature of inhuman systems. There is certainly no black Jesus. In Simon's work, there's not even God.

Emily loves taking complex social problems and exploring them through character-driven stories. She revels in the research—learning everything she can about the issue at hand, a part of the process she doesn't think a lot of people realize is so integral to filmmaking. Ultimately, Emily wants people to leave her films inspired to reflect on their own lives, their own decisions and behaviors. She says, "I think the best kind of activism, the best kind of films really, inspires people to help themselves. That's what I want my work to do."

"I NEVER CRIED ON SET," Emily tells me proudly, describing how difficult shooting *Toe to Toe* was. "The crew used to call me 'the boxer,' because I fought so hard for my vision of this film."

She describes in visceral detail the experience of watching the footage in the editing room and hearing herself fight: "I can hear the cinematographer and AD [assistant director] telling me, 'You don't really need that shot.' Then I say, 'Wait, give me a second.' And I'm sitting there in the editing room, praying that I didn't give in. I'm telling myself, 'It's your baby. You're the only one who will see it through from start to finish. Come on, Em.' And then I hear myself respond, 'No, we need the shot. Let's delay lunch.' And I hear some of the crew groaning, but I feel like cheering."

Directing a film sounds like marshalling an army when you hear Emily talk about it. And as with military culture, a female leader—especially one so determined to get the shot right, even if it means working through lunch—isn't always respected by crews. "I knew some of them thought I was a bitch," Emily says. "You can almost hear the crew talking behind your back, but you get over that pretty quickly. You have to, if you don't want to give up your vision for the film."

Emily would often take a deep breath on set and say to herself, "This is so hard, but I can do it." She seems to thrive in situations of such adversity, as if she feels at home becoming the fighter, instead of her old days of lusting after them. Now she's the one who struggles to get her story told, who is misunderstood and maligned, who triumphs despite the odds. A meaning of one's own.

And the meaning couldn't be more earned. It's almost miraculous that an independent film ever gets made when you consider the entire process—writing a script that can take years and years to complete; scavenging for funding; hiring the hundreds of people required to actually cast, shoot, edit, and market; finding the right actors (a six-month process for *Toe to Toe*); negotiating their contracts and coordinating their schedules; rehearsing; finding locations; shooting against the setting sun and unexpected weather conditions for twenty-five days; pulling it all together in the editing room (another six months); sending it out to festivals; praying like hell that you actually get in. It takes an almost freakish amount of determination to make it through.

That is, until you are discovered, and then things go from very hard to much easier in a matter of lunches.

EMILY RETURNS FROM L.A. with a whole new perspective on the industry. "It's truly the most elite world I've ever been in," she says.

"More elite than the Ivy League?" I ask, thinking about her husband's recent foray into the hiring process at an incredibly select level.

"Well, funny you say that, because most of the producers and production company execs actually are Ivy League grads," she answers. "They're all these totally fascinating, really smart people. They love *The Wire*. They are really interested in social issues. . . . Doesn't mean they can always make films like that, but they're definitely interested."

"That's great," I tell her. "So the meetings went well?"

"Yeah, I genuinely vibed with a bunch of them. I don't know how it will all shake out, but it was nice to just be there and making the connections. It's taken me a while to get in those rooms, so I'm honored to be there."

Emily's agency is throwing a lot of different potential projects her way, including a Queen Latifah picture that includes a quintessential gold digger character. "I passed. It would be great to work with Queen Latifah, but I'm not attaching myself to anything with that kind of portrayal of black women," she says. "I have to be really discerning about what I take on right now."

The project she's really excited about would be a script on charter schools. The production company has no writer yet. Emily is champing at the bit to take a stab at creating a modern-day *Lean on Me* that avoids all the usual clichés—flawless white woman swoops in to save the poor black kids from their urban plight (see *Dangerous Minds*). She wants—surprise, surprise—to center it on a fish-out-of-water character, an Asian teacher (based on the chancellor of D.C. public schools, Michelle Rhee) in Alabama's poorest area, and a quirky, complex black kid who brings the levity needed to balance out the weighty subject matter.

Besides plugging away on her politician script, Emily's got another baby in the making. "I'm pregnant," she tells me, smiling from ear to ear. I give her a huge hug.

EMILY HAS BEEN INVITED to teach a workshop at One on One, a members-only "training and networking studio for professional actors" on Twenty-seventh Street. Eleven actors, ten of them women, sit on black metal folding chairs along three walls in a cozy, carpeted room. Emily sits on an office chair with wheels and listens as they each explain why they got into acting:

"It's my dream to be an actress. It's all it's ever been. All it ever will be."

"I was in the Peace Corps in West Africa, and it made me realize how lucky we are as Americans to do whatever we want to do. When I came back, I knew it was my duty to follow my dream of being an actor."

"Acting, for me, is like falling in love."

I'm impressed at Emily's capacity to keep a straight face. Normally this is the kind of melodrama that would set her off. But she's infinitely kind and encouraging when it comes to other people's dreams.

After the introductions are over, Emily gives a short talk on her philosophy of directing: "Mostly I try to get out of your way. 90 percent of our job happens during casting." She tells them that preparation is critical—an actor must really research the world that his or her character comes from.

One woman says, "I'm really lucky to have a great agent who sends me on lots of auditions, so I tend to try out three or four times a week. I'm also working, of course, to pay the bills, so I find that I don't have a tremendous amount of time to research every part that I'm going for. Do you take that into account?"

"I don't give a shit," Emily replies, startling the room with her tough-love side. "I don't mean to be harsh, but whatever you have to do to get to that place of authenticity with the character, you have to do it. It's game time, and there are a hundred other girls who are hungry for the part in line behind you."

Emily talks about working with Sonequa Martin and Louisa Krause, the two teenage girls in *Toe to Toe*. She had them each write a whole past life for their characters before shooting—"It imbues the performance with this deeper meaning." She also gave Louisa lots of homework—articles from *New York* magazine on sex addiction and books on teenage promiscuity.

"There are lots of images of fast and furious teenage girls on TV," Emily says. "I wanted to get at what was behind that. The trick is to get the social message in there, but put the story first. You have to avoid being didactic or preachy." Both were criticisms that Emily received while in film school.

After the actors ask Emily a few more questions about her process, they set up some chairs at the front of the room and prepare to rehearse a short scene from *Toe to Toe*. It's a fairly significant one in the film, but the actors haven't seen it, so they fly fairly blind. They're surprisingly fluid with the lines, if a bit emotionally messy. When they finish, Emily says, "Good job, guys!"

Then she asks the main actor a series of questions: "How well do you know him? How are you feeling about what's going on with your daughter? What do you want to get out of the conversation?" The woman sits up straighter as she answers Emily's questions, as if they've given her a more solid backbone.

As someone who's never seen this side of filmmaking, I'm amazed at how intuitive the directing process is. It depends so heavily on reading what's missing from the performance and then getting the actor to realize the gaps and internalize the shifts via strategic questioning.

The full dimensions of Emily Abt have shown up in this small room—her tough-love side and her sometimes hidden capacity for empathy and gentleness. She needs all of it to be a good director, to make a good film. Emily is, as she claims, a fighter. But she also hasn't lost the social worker within. She just shows up for different clients these days.

Though most of the actors gave hokey, stock answers when asked why they got involved in the work in the first place, one woman said something that resonated: "After I see a really amazing film, I'm never the same again. When I meet the writer or director of that film, I want to say, 'You have changed me forever.' That's how films change the world."

Emily's face lit up, as if all the struggle has been worth it.

It Ain't Easy Being Green

Nia Martin-Robinson,
environmental justice advocate,
Washington, D.C., via Detroit

Nia's phone rang as she was stumbling around her hotel room, trying to get ready. "Yeah?" she said, holding the cell between her shoulder and her ear as she pulled on her shoe.

Her friend launched right in. "Nia, you're not going to believe this."

"What?"

"You're banned from the convention. Your face, I kid you not, is plastered up next to the entrance with a giant X through it."

"Damn!" Nia had known she was in trouble, but she didn't realize she was in *that* much trouble. The day before, she had been hanging around outside one of the meeting rooms at the eleventh conference of the United Nations Climate Change Convention, where some of the U.S. delegates were speaking on a panel, when a security guard approached her and asked to see what was in the Christmas gift bag she was carrying.

Nia and a small group of other environmental justice activists were going to present the U.S. delegates with a gift of all the things they would need as the planet continues to warm, including an inflatable inner tube, a face mask, an inhaler, and a can of meat. The United States refused to honor the Kyoto

Protocol—an international agreement on climate change up for ratification in 2005.

Apparently you were supposed to register your actions (seems to take all the fun out of it, doesn't it?). Further, the security guard decided that perhaps Nia's intention was to, as she put it, "chuck some Spam at somebody's head." He called in backup—armed guards and even Barbara Black, the Climate Change Convention's NGO (nongovernmental organization) liaison.

Nia was indignant. Security had already told her she had to take off her button that electronically counted down the time remaining in Bush's term. Now they were accusing her of using canned meat as a weapon. Black said to her, "This is completely irresponsible. You can't just do an action whenever you feel like it. This is childish and immature."

"Is it?" Nia responded. "Well, then, my attitude reflects my country's leadership."

As Nia recounts this story, she admits, "That didn't go over so well." Her bag was confiscated, and though she wasn't asked to leave, she could feel suspicious eyes on her for the rest of the day. Apparently they'd decided to ban her from all UN proceedings for the rest of her life, in addition to slapping her picture up at the entrance for all ten thousand participants that year to see.

The next morning, when Nia arrived at the Palais des congrès de Montréal, the convention center where the meeting was taking place, she stayed in the lobby while her friends worked it out. The UN said that the United States kicked her out. The United States said the UN kicked her out. "How does that look, for the U.S. to be silencing one of its own citizens?" Nia asked. Six hours of negotiating later, she was let back in.

Nia's middle name is, appropriately, Eshu—in Yoruba mythology, an orisha (deity or spirit) known as the negotiator. Eshu is also known for playing tricks in order to cultivate maturation in people.

———

NIA MARTIN-ROBINSON, age twenty-nine, isn't your average environmentalist. She can't stand hiking, doesn't own a pair of Tevas, and refuses to camp without a full-size blow-up mattress and a bathroom nearby. In fact, you're most likely to find her in a city setting—she was born and raised in Detroit, just as it was dying a slow, industrial death, and currently lives in Washington, D.C. She often wears khakis and a button-up shirt or a cardigan, nails manicured, hair straightened and curling under her chin.

You might expect a girl like Nia—one burdened and gifted with the heavy weight of African American history (Mom is a radical, Dad a child of the deep South, pre–civil rights legislation)—to find herself involved in antiracist organizing, or maybe working as a civil rights lawyer. But the new vanguard of African American activists—the ones who came of age in the eighties, with hip-hop, Rodney King, and Earth Day—often choose to honor their history through definitively modern movements. Nia is an advocate for environmental justice because, as she puts it, "I grew up in the shadow of a toxic incinerator, in a city with one of the highest pediatric lead poisoning rates and an extremely high asthma rate. Nature is great, but that's not why I'm in this. I'm in this for my people."

She continues, "I think I'm here on this earth to do a small piece of goodness and hope that it can have some type of collective impact. Plain and simple."

Nia is currently doing her "small piece of goodness" as the director of the Environmental Justice and Climate Change Initiative (EJCC), a coalition that, since its founding in 2001, has been committed to reframing the debate in this country about climate change. For too long, environmentalism in general and climate change specifically have been seen as issues applicable or of interest only to white, hybrid-driving hiker types. But this mainstream conception of who cares about and is affected by climate change masks a far more complex story.

Low-income people of color in the United States are, or will be, disproportionately affected by climate change. Part of the reason is geography—80 percent of people of color live in coastal regions, and most are concentrated in urban centers in the South and other areas with substandard air quality. Air pollution, as a result, hits people of color especially hard; 57 percent of whites, 65 percent of African Americans, and 80 percent of Latinos live in 437 counties with substandard air quality. Global warming is expected to double the number of cities with pollutants above the maximum level allowed by national air quality standards. Data gathered by the EJCC also shows that compared to whites, people of color are twice as likely to die in a heat wave, three times more likely to be hospitalized or die from asthma and other respiratory illnesses linked to air pollution, and twice as likely to be uninsured, making it difficult to get help for the health complications caused by environmental degradation.

New Orleans is the environmental justice movement's Little Rock. The images of black folks floating along the streets of the Lower Ninth Ward on makeshift rafts or camping out on roofs, waving distress flags, became undeniable symbols of what can happen to low-income people concentrated in areas vulnerable to natural disasters. And while the severity of Hurricane Katrina can't be decisively blamed on global warming, the Pew Center on Global Climate Change clearly explains the link:

> Because hurricanes draw strength from heat in ocean surface waters, warming the water should generate more powerful hurricanes. Case in point: while Katrina was strengthening from a tropical storm to a category 5 hurricane . . . the surface waters in the Gulf of Mexico were unusually warm. . . . It is no surprise that Katrina became a very powerful storm. While there is no method to determine whether global warming played a role, it is reasonable to say it increased

the probability that the Gulf surface water would be unusually warm on any given day, as it was on August 29 when Katrina's intensity peaked.

Regardless of how much the warming of the Gulf of Mexico emboldened Hurricane Katrina, the more fundamental lesson is this: when disaster strikes, low-income people, usually of color, are the least prepared to evacuate, the least equipped to find a new residence, and the least protected by federal and even non-profit disaster relief agencies.

This is a particularly potent time for the environmental justice movement, not just because Hurricane Katrina put the issues in stark relief, but because the new administration has finally put climate change on the agenda. As I get to know Nia, her time is dominated by discussions about, analysis of, and advocacy concerning the proposed American Clean Energy and Security Act of 2009 (ACES), also known as the Waxman-Markey comprehensive energy bill. As she describes it, "The policy work is tedious. One step forward. Twenty-two steps back."

The new legislation includes a cap-and-trade global warming reduction plan designed to reduce economy-wide greenhouse gas emissions 17 percent by 2020. Other provisions include new renewable requirements for utilities, studies and incentives regarding new carbon capture and sequestration technologies, energy efficiency incentives for homes and buildings, and grants for green jobs, among other things.

Sounds pretty good to the untrained ear, but Nia feels otherwise. In a faux official voice, she says, "Congress is in the midst of trying to pass historic and monumental climate legislation." Then, dropping the act, she exclaims, "That bill is garbage! Are you kidding me? Science is telling us that the U.S. needs to reduce carbon emissions by at least eighty percent below 1990 levels by 2050. This bill calls for reductions to 2005 levels. In order to stabilize our climate, we need to get to 350 parts per million of carbon in the atmosphere. That bill gets us to 450. I'm waiting for the next draft to come out."

It's trademark Nia—no-holds-barred honesty followed by data. She knows her stuff and she's not afraid to say it. Where and when she gets to speak her truth is another story. Though it is one of the few organizations on the Hill devoted to amplifying the voices of people of color and the issues affecting them, the EJCC rarely gets a seat at the official table (mostly populated by big green groups like the World Wildlife Federation, Environmental Defense Fund, National Wildlife Federation, and National Resources Defense Council, along with some labor unions, a few faith-based groups, and, of course, industry).

Nia says, "Mainstream environmental organizations, who it seems would be our most natural allies at the table, have historically ignored the issues of our communities. Some are trying to diversify themselves in an effort to *look* diverse. Others are genuinely interested in what's happening in people of color and low-income communities. But there's a ton of them that have taken a very defeatist attitude, that this is the best bill we're going to get. They're putting money into it, making commercials, you name it."

Nia's frustration over the bill, and the "enviros" that support it, is palpable. I ask her if she thinks she's being too idealistic; after all, isn't it better to get a weak bill rather than no bill at all?

She's quick to answer, having obviously met this point of view before in her travels around D.C. "The way I see it, there's urgency, and then there's life and death. The big thing right now for the enviros is making sure that we have a bill by Copenhagen [the 2009 UN Climate Conference]. Domestic legislation or not, we need to go into Copenhagen ready to negotiate and not be the bastards we've been for the last eight years."

She goes on, growing more emphatic: "But our communities

aren't only worried about Copenhagen. We need to make sure that there are no hot spots, that there are real reductions in emissions, that money is being put back into the community, that we're investing in solutions that not only break our dependence on foreign oil but on fossil fuels, period. Issues around climate change, for us, are life and death. They go past urgency to the well-being of our children. It's hard to compromise from that place."

AS I WALK DOWN Sixteenth Street NW in Washington, D.C., on a warm May morning, I watch hurried people in business suits piling into buses headed downtown and marvel at all the embassies along the route to Nia's office. Though we've spoken on the phone, we've never met. I'm looking forward to putting a face to that spirited voice.

When I finally zero in on what should be the EJCC office, I find a big yellow brick cathedral with ornate molding and a carved, contented Jesus staring down at me from the top of the front door. I look around for a bit, wondering if I mixed up the numbers, before deciding to give Nia a call. She answers and says she'll be right down to let me in. The church rents space to the U.S. Climate Action Network, which rents a corner to the EJCC. Nia works in a large room with lots of natural light flooding in from big square windows. She's got an L-shaped wooden desk in one corner, with framed pictures of her family perched near her computer monitor. The shelves nearby are mostly empty, except for a few cardboard boxes filled with literature. This is clearly a small operation. The Web site lists two other staff members, but they work remotely.

Nia is scheduled to stop by the Energy Action Coalition office today, field a call from the Congressional Black Caucus, and go to a green jobs meeting at the Department of the Interior. I'll tag along to see a D.C. insider-outsider in action. But first we talk about the origins of both Nia and the environmental justice movement.

"What is your first memory of social justice activism?" I ask Nia.

She nods her head and launches right in. "I remember African American students did a sit-in at Wayne State because they wanted an African American studies program. My mother took food and water to the students. I must have been about six years old. I remember being very upset, because I wanted to stay and spend the night. It was exciting. There was all this energy."

Dissent is in Nia's DNA. Her mother, Jacqueline, a self-described Pan-Africanist, has been preaching about the benefits of breast-feeding, talking about the country's dirty history of eugenics, and raging against the injustice of U.S. economic policy, both domestic and foreign, since the seventies.

Another of Nia's most formative memories is that of her mom's vigilante research into the International Monetary Fund and the World Bank and her subsequent field trip to their official headquarters. Jacqueline marched right in and made both of her daughters, Nia and her younger sister, Shae, carry giant bags that she soon filled with reports and brochures that she picked up.

"What was she trying to find?" I ask Nia.

"She was just collecting pamphlets to see how they were talking about themselves. She got all kinds of reports. We thought it was just crap, girl," Nia says, laughing. Looking back, Nia is grateful that her mom taught her about these institutions—two that would later be part of her almost daily conversations—when she was so young. Her mom instilled in her the notion that these powerful organizations were as much her business as anybody else's. When Nia stops giggling she goes on, "That is where my mom's activism is its strongest. She is always learning, always researching, always trying to understand things." Jacqueline is now in the process of getting her PhD from Wayne State University in qualitative analysis, with a cognate in community medicine.

Nia's father, Alvin, also has roots in dissent. He was born

in Meridian, Mississippi, in 1950 and grew up sneaking into St. John's Baptist Church so he could hear the grown-ups talking about these important things called "civil rights" and even, once, hear Dr. Martin Luther King Jr. preach a gospel of liberation. Nia was baptized in that church, just inches from where Dr. King once stood to inspire the folks of Meridian to imagine a better Mississippi.

Nia says, "My dad always emphasized reading and education, because he grew up in a city where little black boys didn't have access to things. He graduated high school and was immediately drafted into Vietnam." Alvin didn't talk much about Vietnam with his kids, other than to tell them about a dog he adopted while he was over there. He named it, well, Dog. His eyes grew glossy when he talked about Dog's untimely death down in a tunnel.

When Alvin was asked to go down in the tunnels to look for Vietcong, he made a practice of going just far enough to disappear from sight, roll around, and come out looking dirty. He ran into the enemy only once. "What did you do, Daddy?" Nia asked him.

"I killed that motherfucker," he responded without hesitation.

When he came back home, war protestors called him a baby-killer. Nia says, "He resented the sentiment. After all, they'd been killing people that looked like my daddy in Mississippi for years." Alvin moved to Detroit, met Nia's mother, and became a fireman. They had two children together—Nia and Shae—before separating in 1989 and eventually divorcing in 2003.

Things were always pretty amicable, although Jacqueline and Alvin did worry about their oldest daughter. Jacqueline thought that Alvin's unchecked cursing was giving her a foul mouth. Alvin worried that Jacqueline's tender heart was making Nia too sensitive.

Nia has a vivid memory of being about four years old and seeing Kermit the Frog admit, "It ain't easy being green," during an episode of *Sesame Street*. She burst into tears. She explains, "I just internalized this pain from him. My mom talked me through the song, but it just sounded so sad. In my mind, he was green and he couldn't help it. It was like when people were mean to black people."

Nia reports that she had horrible self-esteem in elementary and middle school, but eventually came into her own in high school, where she became a social butterfly. "I was always really smart," she says, "but I was also a classic underachiever and a real procrastinator." It's not hard to imagine. Nia is perpetually laid-back. She walks slowly. She likes to shoot the shit. She's far from a type A personality.

She entered public high school with about 1,200 kids and graduated with 562. The class of 1998 was on record for having the largest loss from freshman to senior year in the history of the school. Nia went on to Wayne State, only to drop out after two and half years as a pre–physical therapy major. "If I had done a little bit more self-application," Nia speculates, "I would probably be a Harvard graduate right now."

"So do you regret it?" I ask.

"Nope. The way that life happens is very specific. I made decisions in high school that led me to Wayne State and allowed me to be in Detroit and start working in environmental justice. I got exposed to ideas around the intersection of race and class and climate, and now I'm here," Nia says. "Don't get me wrong. I want to go back to school eventually—but for me. I don't regret any of my choices. I feel like I'm at the place in my life where I'm doing the work I was meant to do. I don't know that taking any other path would have gotten me to this place."

ELIZA SIMON, THE MANAGING DIRECTOR of the Energy Action Coalition, hands Nia and me cupcakes and sits down in a chair across from us. The inside of this D.C. brownstone is abuzz

with mostly white kids in their twenties and barely thirties—
G-chatting, eating late lunch out of Tupperware containers, and
drinking from stainless steel water bottles.

Much like the Environmental Justice and Climate Change
Initiative, the Energy Action Coalition serves to unite a range of
organizations under one banner, in their case a "youth clean and
just energy movement." There are over fifty organizational partners, including the EJCC, representing over a hundred thousand
young people, and they are responsible for hosting the Power
Shift Conference—the epicenter of youth-led environmental
activism. According to the Energy Action Coalition, in 2009 an
astounding twelve thousand young people showed up.

"So, Nia can be challenging," Eliza says, smiling mischievously at Nia, who is on the couch beside me. They clearly have
a playful relationship—two strong women with very different
styles who have an understanding and appreciation for one another. Nia asks about Eliza's pet rabbit and upcoming wedding.
Eliza tells me glowing things about her friend.

"Tell the truth, girl," Nia says.

"She keeps people honest to the commitment to racial justice
within climate change," Eliza clarifies, taking a little taste of her
icing. "I mean, if we're in a meeting and she thinks that perspective is missing, she'll say something. Sometimes people can take
that the wrong way. I've heard people say, 'Nia is in there acting
like a real bitch.'" Nia chuckles.

Eliza goes on, "But the truth is, Nia just has an impressive
capacity to explain and convey her passion for environmental
justice. That passion might intimidate people, but they at least
get it when she's done speaking."

Eliza and Nia agree that while the environmental movement,
as a whole, is still struggling to incorporate a sound race- and
class-based analysis into its work, the youth movement is a few
steps ahead. It's not a perfect model, but it's a model nonetheless.

The Energy Action Coalition is deliberately trying to diversify its staff and court more organization partners from the environmental justice world—in part thanks to Nia's interventions.

"Aren't you going to tell her how funny I am?" Nia asks.

"She's honestly one of the funniest people I know," Eliza says. "And I'm not just saying that to please her. She can talk herself into or out of any situation."

"What do you think is on the horizon for Nia?" I ask.

Eliza pauses, reflecting for a few moments. She smiles over at Nia, generously, as if she's envisioning her bedecked in a crown and holding a royal staff. "I don't know, but I know she'll keep running things."

IN 2000, HAVING LEFT Wayne State, Nia was working for the city of Detroit as a recreation leader at the Parks and Recreation Department. Her boss at the time recognized Nia's talent for engaging people and encouraged her to apply for a position at Detroiters Working for Environmental Justice (DWEJ).

Nia felt like she had finally found herself at DWEJ. Her supervisor, Donele Wilkins, initiated her into the overlapping worlds of environmental justice and community organizing. Nia felt effective, respected. She served as the program assistant for the Community Action against Asthma project and also got to serve as the youth rep at conferences. In October 2001, Donele took Nia to the Second National People of Color Environmental Leadership Summit—a meeting packed with all of the best and brightest minds of the environmental justice movement from all over the country. Nia was inspired: "It was over after that."

It was at the summit that she learned about the short but fascinating history of the environmental justice movement. Its genesis is often pegged to protests in 1982 to stop a PCB disposal site from being opened in Warren County, North Carolina. Despite the fact that sixteen thousand people from the surrounding area—75 percent African American—marched against the site, it opened. The silver lining was that the environmental justice movement was officially born.

But Nia also points out that the civil rights movement was deeply intertwined in environmental concerns, even if they weren't always framed that way. Dr. King, for example, was killed while fighting for the rights of sanitation workers. At the time it was largely seen as a labor and equality issue, but it was also profoundly environmental. The sanitation workers wanted to be protected from disease-causing toxins, in addition to being paid a fair wage.

Much of the most potent environmental justice work has taken place in the South—for good reason. In 1983, the United States General Accounting Office conducted a study of several Southern states that found three out of every four landfills were located near predominantly minority communities. In 1987, a report by the United Church of Christ Commission for Racial Justice showed that the most significant factor in determining hazardous waste facility sites, nationwide, was race. The study also found that three out of every five African Americans and Hispanics live in communities bordering on unregulated toxic waste sites. From there the environmental justice movement developed through grassroots actions throughout the fifty states, punctuated by the occasional national summit or conference.

It's an interesting movement, because it's intentionally local and invested in community-oriented, small-scale actions— defeating a local referendum for a new coal plant, getting a stream or a lake cleaned up, educating a neighborhood about the dangers of asbestos or lead. Though the movement has become more unified in recent years, you can still find environmental justice activists all over the nation doing similar work while having little knowledge of one another.

Thus the importance of coalitions like the one Nia runs. The

Environmental Justice and Climate Change Initiative brings disparate U.S. organizations—from the Intertribal Council on Utility Policy to the Black Leadership Forum to the Church of the Brethren—together as one united front to influence national policy and the next generation of environmentalists. Nia landed at the EJCC after leaving DWEJ to do labor organizing with Service Employees International Union for a couple of years.

Even during her time organizing home child-care and health workers, she was active on the steering committee of the EJCC. When the director position opened up, she had to do some soul-searching. It would mean a major salary cut and a move to D.C. She'd never really thought of herself being on the Hill. But despite all her reservations, she jumped on the chance. "Environmental justice work was always calling me," she says.

NIA AND THE WOMAN from the Congressional Black Caucus (CBC), Irene Schwoeffermann, start the conference call talking about their hair. The D.C. summer is right around the corner, and both are trying to get their hair taken care of before the oppressive humidity has its way with it. "It's too hard to do all the work we do and stay beautiful at the same time," Nia says, totally serious.

"Basically," agrees Irene. She is the coalitions director of the CBC, a committee with forty-two members founded in 1971 and designed to "promote the public welfare through legislation designed to meet the needs of millions of neglected citizens." Nia thinks that Irene, young and ambitious, is going places.

Nia gets down to business: "I was really happy with the CBC letter."

"Yay," cheers Irene. The letter essentially summarized the CBC's position on, and hopes for, the new climate change legislation.

Nia continues, "It was great to read it, especially right now, feeling like the Waxman bill is, I can be frank with you, garbage.

I don't know what's going to happen in markup. I'm hearing all kinds of things, but I don't really know what's going on."

"How closely have you been following it?"

"Fairly closely. I've been trying to keep my ear to the street. I've really been looking at how some of the other enviros are thinking and feeling about it. The one thing I did hear, that was quite startling, was that there was going to be a serious reduction in the targets, which were already low, which is why I was so glad that the CBC letter set the targets that it set."

"Does EJCC have a formal evaluation of the bill?" Irene asks.

"I'm working on that right now," Nia says.

I'm skeptical. Nia's gift of gab doesn't seem complemented by a penchant for paperwork.

She says, "A lot of EJ groups are very pro–carbon tax. It's been a struggle inside of EJCC to have this conversation, but what I keep telling them—in my Washington, D.C., reality, a cap-and-trade bill is probably what we're going to get. It's really important to me that we, as EJ people, as people representing those disproportionately affected, have an opportunity to participate in this cap-and-trade conversation. Period. Some of us could hold out for a carbon tax, but at the end of the day we need to be a part of making sure that we get the best bill possible for our community."

Suddenly, the usually uncompromising Nia seems downright strategic. It's all relative in the end. Among the big green groups, she's a bold, outsider voice, shouting about the life-or-death situation that poor people of color face when it comes to climate change; among her own people, she's an insider trying to translate the intricacies and inevitable disappointments of D.C. compromises. The goal is always the same: brown the green agenda.

———

IT WAS A SUNNY SATURDAY, 1978, in Detroit, Michigan. The farmers' market was bustling with people browsing baskets spilling over with fruits and vegetables from nearby farms—red peppers, jalapeños, apples, heads of lettuce. Jacqueline Sia Robinson was dressed so she could feel what little breeze there was against her skin—flowing dress and sandals, her silver bangles clanking against one another as she brought a shiny, ripe tomato to her nose to smell. She set it down and kept moving.

Alvin Martin, a young man in a sports car the same color as her unchosen tomato, drove by just then. He spotted this beautiful woman—her style, her curves, her pride—and hollered out the window the first thing that popped into his head: "I'll take you to Africa, girl!"

Jacqueline smiled in spite of herself. A glimmer in her eye appeared.

Though Nia's parents divorced long ago, when they greet each other at the Olive Garden on Van Dyke on a rainy Thursday evening in Detroit, hugging and sitting on a bench in the lobby, you can sense that they have a profound respect for one another. Nia, despite the requisite eye-rolling and embarrassed facial expressions, is obviously enamored of both of them. She's corralled her entire family—mom, dad, sister, and half-sister, Allina—to come together and meet me.

As we wait for a table, they all paw through the gifts that Nia has brought back for them from South Africa—a couple of tapestries for Shae, a bag and a necklace for Allina, coffee and a photo book of beautiful black-and-white jazz prints for Alvin, and a Sangoma doll and some CDs for Jacqueline. Jacqueline, who has short, bouncy dreads and a small silver nose ring, eyes Alvin's coffee. "You know I love coffee, Nia! Why'd you bring that for your daddy?"

"I drink tea now," Alvin says quietly, proudly. "Peach Tranquility." He wears a pair of stonewashed jeans and a navy tank top that reads DETROIT FIRE DEPT. Nia made him promise he wouldn't wear anything with holes.

The girls all laugh at their father—a tiny, taut man among a clan of tall, big-hipped, big-breasted women. "You put your finger up like this, Daddy?" Shae asks, pretending to be a snooty tea drinker lifting her pinky as she takes a sip from her imaginary cup of tea.

"I don't do teahouses. I don't do poetry readings," Alvin says with a stern look on his face, as if reclaiming some of his manhood.

When we sit down, Jacqueline launches right in: "So what do you want to know? Did she tell you that she sat on Assata Shakur's lap? Did she tell you that she has a personal letter from Amiri Baraka's son?"

The girls laugh again. "What are you laughing at?" Jacqueline asks them. "I've already had two meetings today. I'm tired."

"You got any nice left?" Nia asks.

Jacqueline pretends to look in the pocket of her black blazer, then says, "Not much. You girls better watch out."

I ask Jacqueline about a story Nia told me. Apparently, Jacqueline was hanging out with some friends and decided to Google her amazing activist daughter to show off. Nia's Twitter feed came up first thing and, to Jacqueline's horror, it read: "I'm too fucking emotional right now." The next time that Jacqueline and Nia spoke on the phone, she let her have it.

"Look," says Jacqueline, explaining her worries to me, "I'm my daughters' biggest fan. Period. I will do anything and everything I can to ensure that they succeed. If some employer Googles Nia, I don't want that being the first thing that comes up."

Alvin jumps in. "Nia's always been too sensitive."

"What do you mean?" I ask.

"She's too caring. Always has been. You gotta be tough in this world, or people will take advantage of you." Right as he says this, Nia hands her drink over to her little sister because she didn't like what she ordered. "You see what I mean?" he asks, motioning toward the hand-off. Nia says nothing.

We all order rich pasta dishes, and the conversation wanders to the girls' childhood memories, eBay auctions, and Alvin's most recent breakup with a woman they all liked. This is a family that knows how to laugh together. I look around and wonder whether some of the families sitting in bored silence at other tables are jealous of this crew, if they ache to pull up a chair and join in all the fun.

I'm not surprised by the wit and the laughter. What does throw me for a loop is how quiet Nia is around her family. It's as if Nia channels her family's energy everywhere she goes—their bold declarations, edgy humor, and self-assuredness—and then as soon as she's with them, she becomes the empathic, fragile one. It seems like more than a function of family roles. It's almost as if Nia's deepest self is this sensitive, quiet soul, but she feels the luxury of letting that out only in the company of her family.

As dinner winds to a close, Jacqueline looks me straight in the eyes and says, "Nia could do anything."

"That's right," says Alvin, nodding his bald head in agreement. "Nia can do anything she wants to do. She's just got to work on not being so sensitive, like her mother." Jacqueline rolls her eyes at him and says, "Oh, shut up, old man," with a smile on her face.

As we make our way out of the restaurant and into the parking lot, I see Alvin squeeze Nia sweetly and give her a giant kiss on the cheek: "Love you, baby."

"Love you too, Daddy," Nia says.

Before Jacqueline gets into her car, I spy Alvin hand her the coffee from South Africa.

THE ENVIRONMENTAL JUSTICE MOVEMENT has gained a lot of media attention as of late through media darlings like MacArthur

Fellowship winner Majora Carter, originally of the nonprofit Sustainable South Bronx, and Van Jones, founder of Green for All, ousted from his role as Obama's special advisor for green jobs after some controversial past remarks hit the airwaves.

Nia knows both and respects their work, although she is weary of the ways in which the media spin on the issue tends to emphasize job opportunities rather than justice. "The green job conversation has ghettoized climate change work in many respects," she says. "Now you have big green groups and politicians who only want to engage people of color about green jobs."

Indeed, Jones makes the argument in his book *The Green Collar Economy* that the dual crises of socioeconomic inequality and environmental destruction can be fixed with one solution: "a new green economy—one with the power to lift people out of poverty while respecting and repairing the environment."

He writes, "We are entering an era during which our very survival will demand invention and innovation on a scale never before seen in the history of human civilization. Only the business community has the requisite skills, experience, and capital to meet that need."

Nia worries that the green jobs hype is a spuriously simple solution for what amounts to a far more complex problem. "Sure, we can install solar panels in the suburbs, but then big business is still putting coal-fired power plants in our backyard," she says. "What good does that do us? We need to see the holistic picture of this crisis."

This kind of thinking characterizes Nia's activism at every step. She's less interested in strategy than she is in equality, less motivated by approval than by outrage. Whereas Jones seems hell-bent on presenting environmental solutions that feel politically safe, Nia isn't afraid to make people in power uncomfortable.

Interestingly, in his 2009 *New Yorker* profile, Jones is quoted as saying, "You may eventually wind up with a more pure outcome, like a Gandhi or a Mandela, but no young radical is running around with pure motives. I certainly wasn't motivated only by love for the people. I was trying to find some kind of community, or some kind of sense of belonging, or some sense of redemption through heroic deeds. I wasn't being honest with myself about it, and it all just proved to be incredibly fragile."

Nia seems to contradict that notion. It's not that she isn't self-interested; when I first approached her about being in the book, she said, "Is this my Oprah moment?" After laughing, she clarified, "I think that we work tirelessly, often for little to nothing, and we deserve recognition." We both knew she was talking about herself. Nia would like to make more money. She'd like to travel the world. She'd like to win fancy awards.

But what motivates her really does seem rather pure. Beneath all the tough talk and the environmental know-how is that little girl, crying at Kermit's song while watching *Sesame Street*.

Class Action

Tyrone Boucher, radical philanthropist, Philadelphia

I wait by the Mahatma Gandhi statue in Union Square as the sounds of an urban farmers' market buzz around me—crates of vegetables being lifted from truck beds, a guy hawking newspapers by the subway entrance, a conversation between two organic farmers. It seems an apt place to meet Tyrone Boucher for the first time. He's the cofounder, with activist lawyer Dean Spade, of a blog called Enough, "a space for conversations about how a commitment to wealth redistribution plays out in our lives," and he's currently investing time and energy in food politics—working at a small-scale cooperative called Mariposa, in West Philadelphia.

I stumbled on his blog months earlier and was shocked at how transparent Tyrone, age twenty-six, was—he posted his entire giving plan and a thoughtful letter to his father about his reasoning for giving away the $400,000 he inherited. He's part of a larger movement of young people from wealthy families who are questioning the morality of wealth accumulation and pioneering new ways of what they call "social justice philanthropy."

The timing couldn't be better: the United States is currently experiencing the biggest intergenerational transfer of wealth in its history. The Social Welfare Research Institute at Boston College estimates that even with the recent economic recession, $41 trillion will be inherited during the fifty-five-year period from

1998 through 2052. But the huge amount of wealth being passed down is concentrated in very few hands. According to the *Christian Science Monitor*, only 24 percent of adult Americans expect to get an inheritance, and those who do can expect to receive an average of only $37,700. Tyrone's experience is rare, but it also means that what he does with his inheritance—and what other young people like him do—can have a significant impact on all of us.

After e-mailing back and forth a bit, Tyrone and I found a time when he would be in New York to see his partner. We didn't bother exchanging phone numbers or physical descriptions. I put two and two together and figured Tyrone was probably a black gay guy in his twenties.

When a white trans kid, wearing black jeans cuffed at the ankle and a short-sleeved button-down shirt, walks up and says shyly, sweetly, "Courtney?" I am totally stunned—confronted with my own taken-for-granted assumption. In fact, it takes me a minute to even become conscious of how stunned I look. Tyrone has a punk rock aesthetic, his playfully curving eyebrows erupting into little unruly tufts at both centers, and tattooed lines on two fingers of his hands. He emanates gentleness.

"Hi," I say, eventually replacing my shock with a smile. "So good to meet you."

TYRONE DOESN'T MIND surprising people. In fact, his young life has been composed of a series of experiments in not meeting people's expectations. Unlike so many privileged kids of our generation—known for its dutifulness—Tyrone has consistently rejected the rules put on him by a society that he diagnoses as oppressive and unjust. School? Couldn't stand it. Even though he attended the Putney School in Vermont, a place he describes as an "artsy farm high school," he spent most of those years frustrated that he wasn't allowed to do his own thing. He zealously thumbed through the pages of *The Teenage Liberation Handbook: How to Quit School and Get a Real Life and Education*, fantasizing about all of the exciting projects he could undertake if he wasn't stuck in high school. He loved learning and felt grateful for the amazing art program and nontraditional after-school activities (blacksmithing, gardening, knitting, farming) that his progressive private high school had to offer, but he resented being asked to pour energy into classes he wasn't interested in.

He remembers his state of mind at the time: "I know deep down in the depths of my being that I just don't give a shit about school. And that's fine with me."

What he did give a shit about was the DIY (do it yourself) punk subculture that he became immersed in during high school—a culture that nurtured independent production of music, zines, and art and encouraged independent thinking and creativity. This community was where he felt most at home. "My early understanding was 'I'm a freak,'" Tyrone says. "I'm not like other kids. I'm queer and a weirdo and I don't fit in." He spent much of his time at shows of obscure punk bands, rocking out alongside friends covered in tattoos, wearing threadbare T-shirts and weathered Carhartts. But it wasn't just about the music; it was about a whole philosophy of life that challenged mainstream norms and strove to build community and culture based on independence from the status quo.

But everything was not as it seemed. Though Tyrone was internally rejecting traditional education, he was also filling out applications for a long list of mostly elite colleges and scoring in the top 1 percent on his SATs. When I ask him about the contradiction—typing out college admissions applications while adoring *The Teenage Liberation Handbook*—he replies, "I was just on autopilot."

The answer doesn't satisfy me. After all, this was a kid hellbent on redefining education, creating his own path, and stepping off the mainstream trajectory defined for him by his family and class upbringing. When I push him on it, he relents. "I think I just sort of thought that if I filled out the applications, then I could keep my dad off my back. I never thought I would actually go to any of the schools I was applying to."

"I WASN'T SUPPOSED TO TELL you this," Tyrone's mom said. Tyrone was flopped on the couch in their airy Vermont farmhouse, thumbing through some zines and chatting with his mom about the future. Graduation was approaching, and Tyrone's dad— divorced from his mom by this time—was hoping that Tyrone would go to one of the colleges that had accepted him. The fat envelopes weighed heavily in Tyrone's mind. He wanted to be free, unencumbered, not sit in more classrooms.

His mom went on, "You have a trust fund. You're going to inherit four hundred thousand dollars when you turn twenty-one."

Tyrone wasn't surprised, exactly—he knew that his father, who lived in a fancy new condo in Austin, was wealthy and generous. It wasn't old money; Tyrone's father made his fortune by cofounding a software company in the family's basement when Tyrone was a baby. So no, it wasn't surprising; but hearing the number out loud, the concrete nature of the tall, proud four and those zeroes, overwhelmed Tyrone. (Of course $400,000, as significant a sum as it is, pales in comparison to the amount of money some kids from wealthy families inherit.)

"The minute I get it, I'm going to give it away," he told his mom.

THAT WAS ACTUALLY THE LAST conversation that Tyrone had about his trust fund for years. He says, "I filed it away."

"Did you file it away effectively?" I ask, imagining Tyrone among a little crew of pierced punks eating pizza from a Domino's dumpster, reveling in their rejection of capitalism and napkins. It seems as if it would have been really hard to compartmentalize.

"I didn't tell people. I didn't talk about it. Nobody talked about their class background—at least not about having privilege," he says.

"It's interesting to me that in a culture built on the idea of not conforming and being deeply vulnerable and honest, it wouldn't come up," I tell him.

"Hence the problem of so much of that subculture," Tyrone admits. "It was cool to act poor. There's no analysis of what it means to actually be poor."

After graduating high school, Tyrone took a year off, during which he got a premier education in adventure. He lived the life of a true vagabond—hitchhiking wherever the wind or a new friend took him, scrounging for food, sleeping outside—until he finally relented and went to Stanford.

"Stanford?" I ask in disbelief. "Of all the schools, Stanford seems like one of the least likely fits for you."

"Exactly," says Tyrone. "I thought it would be a unique experience. Already, in high school, I was so entrenched in my counterculture that I was bored with it. I figured that if I went to a counterculture college, I might be tempted to pretend it was real life." Stanford—with its palm trees bending gracefully beside California mission-style buildings and its sun-kissed lacrosse players laughing on the quad—was a symbol of elitism so pronounced, so obvious, that it didn't feel dangerous to Tyrone. There would be no chance of slipping into conformity when it manifested as keg parties and classes in free-market economics.

Indeed. After just two months, Tyrone left Stanford, never to return.

For the next four years (2001–2005), instead of sitting in the hallowed halls of Stanford, Tyrone continued to travel with his motley community of hitchhiking, train-hopping punks and queers. It was a beautiful, liberating time. Tyrone felt truly independent, while simultaneously surrounded by a loyal community of DIY mavens, anarchists, and dropouts. He felt like the breach that had always gaped uncomfortably large between his values and his lifestyle was being lovingly sewn shut.

But it wasn't utopia. Looking back, Tyrone feels conflicted. "There's part of me that has this reaction—'Oh God, I was so oblivious.' There were so many problematic things about that time," he says, referring to the lack of race and class awareness among many of the punk kids. Indeed, some critics call the white kids that hang out on park benches in San Francisco's Haight neighborhood or play bad music in Washington Square Park "trustafarians"—referring to their unconscious parody of those who come from poorer, darker cultures.

Tyrone staves off the embarrassment by seeing that season of his life for what it really was. "For me, that moment in time, personally, was more about my own liberation from alienation and isolation than about a political awakening."

His awakening unfolded more like a sleepy morning than a burst of sunlight—a radical-women-of-color zine here, a disillusioning conversation there. Every time he would stop at his dad's condo, he would spend hours printing out readings on white supremacy. Peggy McIntosh's essay "White Privilege: Unpacking the Invisible Knapsack"—in which she encourages the reader to examine unearned privileges as minute as easily finding Band-Aids to match your skin tone—had a big impact on Tyrone. He devoured bell hooks and Angela Davis, examining the bibliographies in the back of each of their tomes to determine his next assignment. Tyrone, though not a fan of formal schooling, is a voracious reader and self-motivated learner. More than any other person I profiled for this book, he was constantly recommending books to me.

The readings helped him see his adventures on the road in a harsher light. For several years, Tyrone attended Camp Trans, a big festival in the middle of the woods that was created to challenge the transphobic policy of the Michigan Womyn's Music Festival, a large annual feminist gathering that excludes transgender women. Tyrone reveled in the gender diversity of the participants, but remembers taking a good look around and realizing, "Huh, I hang out with mostly white people, and I always have."

He was also growing increasingly uncomfortable with hiding his wealth. When opportunities came up for new friends to come and stay at his parents' houses, he felt tense. What would they make of his father's aesthetic—all modern, sharp edges, brushed steel, and dark hardwood? What would they think about his mother, just one lone woman, living in such a big farmhouse? "The dissonance between my politics and my class privilege was getting louder and louder in my own head," Tyrone reflects. He had been through the process of coming to terms with his racial privilege. It seemed well past time to do the same with regard to his class privilege.

His motivation was solidified by one particularly difficult conversation that he had with a friend who grew up poor. "How could you turn your back on an opportunity like going to Stanford?" she asked. "Nobody gets that. How can you act like you're above it?"

Tyrone felt like he'd been slapped in the face. He didn't regret leaving Stanford. He knew that he would have been miserable there, that the place would have crushed his spirit, but he did have regrets. "What I find really embarrassing to think about in retrospect," Tyrone says, "was my own arrogance."

THE NEXT TIME WE MEET, Tyrone is talking a mile a minute, bubbling over with excitement about his recent trip to upstate New York to meet "movement elders" David Gilbert and Naomi Jaffe, two key figures from the Weather Underground Organization (WUO)—the militant faction of Students for a Democratic Society. SDS, as it was referred to, was the organizational center of student activism in the sixties. Its methods were disruptive, but generally peaceful—hosting teach-ins against the Vietnam War, protesting corporate recruiting and paternalistic rules on campuses, and coordinating the largest student strike in U.S. history, involving campuses all over the nation, on April 26, 1968.

The WUO, also called the Weathermen, was founded in 1969 by a mostly white faction of SDS members who wanted to develop more militant, underground resistance to U.S. imperialism in solidarity with people of color. In their founding document, *You Don't Need a Weatherman to Know Which Way the Wind Blows*, they established their philosophy: "the main struggle going on in the world today is between U.S. imperialism and the national liberation struggles against it."

Over the next five years or so, the WUO would conduct a campaign of bombings, usually targeted at government buildings; help writer and drug enthusiast Timothy Leary get out of jail; and even issue a "Declaration of a State of War" against the United States government. Naomi Jaffe says, "We felt that doing nothing in a period of repressive violence is itself a form of violence."

The WUO and militant groups like it aimed to protect human life, but in the heat of their militancy, they sometimes failed. On March 6, 1970, three WUO members died in an accidental explosion at their pad in Greenwich Village. And Gilbert is currently serving a sentence of seventy-five years to life for his role in an attempted robbery that ended in the death of two police officers and a security guard in 1981. Tyrone visited Gilbert at the Clinton Correctional Facility, where he's incarcerated. Jaffe, who was never incarcerated, lives in Troy, New York, and is involved with antiracist and feminist organizing. Tyrone was introduced to both of them through a friend.

"It must have been incredible to exist in that political moment, to feel that liberation movements were on the verge of defeating imperialism," he exclaims, referring to the explosive moment in the late sixties and early seventies when the WUO was most active. It's not just the idealism of the day that seems to inspire Tyrone, but the deep commitment of those privileged young people who believed in revolutionary struggle. He often talks about various clandestine activists from the sixties and seventies who supported nationalist liberation movements, both in the United States and globally, risking safety and security because of a deep belief in justice.

In contrast, Tyrone and I sit discussing radical revolution in a place that, on the surface, seems distant from the radical struggle that is the topic of our conversation—the Resource Generation offices, located in the headquarters of the Mertz Gilmore Foundation, a luxury brownstone on East Eighteenth Street in Manhattan. Dan Berger, a young radical, wrote a painstaking history of the WUO, and in it he argues that "privilege was its *raison d'être*—the group set out to use its privilege in service of revolutionary change." Resource Generation (RG)—the very center of the new movement of young radical Americans with privilege, and the organization responsible for Tyrone's class consciousness—has an almost identical raison d'être, but its methodologies manifest very differently. RG organizes young people with wealth to leverage their class privilege for social justice. They don't bomb buildings; they teach workshops, organize conferences, and support young people to have dialogues with their families and communities about class, wealth, and social change.

Tyrone facilitates workshops for RG from time to time, so we are welcome to use their space when we have our interviews. "Something that hits me really hard when I hear about political movements from a few decades ago," Tyrone says, "was that the nonprofit system didn't exist on the left at that time. Things are so different now—I've never known a world before the nonprofit industrial complex."

The term "nonprofit industrial complex" was coined by an organization called INCITE! Women of Color Against Violence—

a collective that was stripped of its Ford Foundation funding after publicly declaring support for Palestinians. INCITE! compiled a collection of essays, considered required reading among the more radical RG folks, called *The Revolution Will Not Be Funded,* published by South End Press in 2007. In it, the authors argue that the nonprofit model "replicates historical oppression by keeping funders in power over activists, emphasizing institution building and business practices over organizing and systemic change, and perhaps most egregious, forcing social justice activists to please their funders rather than their own communities."

Though the rhetoric in the book can sometimes feel hyperbolic, the argument is profound. The development of the nonprofit sector—initiated largely because it would provide a tax haven for the superrich, while also allowing them to do some good—has historically been seen through rose-colored glasses. Philanthropists are routinely celebrated for "making the world a better place"; but if you actually examine where people donate their money, most often it would be more accurate to recognize them for making *their* world a better place. Giving to alma maters and elite cultural organizations, like the ballet or the opera, top most yearly philanthropy lists. The Giving USA Foundation found that dollars donated to groups working most directly with those in poverty dropped from 24 percent of annual philanthropy in 1955 to 8 percent in 2004; organizations that help America's poor are particularly neglected.

The nonprofit sector also has an interesting impact on youth activism. Young people pumped up on altruistic visions log on to Idealist.org, clamoring for nonprofit jobs that seem to be the most direct route to do good. They are quickly assimilated into a system that, more often than not, maintains the status quo whereby wealthy, mostly white people hold institutional power—with the added psychological bonus of getting to feel smug about their charity work. As Tiffany Lethabo King and Ewuare Osayande ask in *The Revolution Will Not Be Funded,* "What are the implications of a social justice movement in which power and resources are transferred based on one's ability to develop a relationship with the right white people?"

Tyrone was already convinced of this critique, but studying radical youth activism of the sixties and seventies seems to have only increased his investment in the idea that the nonprofit system is actually part of the problem. "During that era, there was so much social justice movement stuff happening, and no one who was truly working for fundamental change expected to be paid for their activism."

"Right," I respond. "But isn't there also an inherent elitism in expecting people to be able to do activism without being paid? Wasn't that part of the critique of the radical left movement in the sixties—that they weren't aware of the luxury of protest?"

Tyrone is quick to counter: "The work people do to fight for liberation is different than the work we do to earn a living, and it always has been. There's certainly overlap sometimes, but you have to wonder: why would the capitalist system pay you to fight it? If we're trying to build a mass movement, we need to create social justice infrastructure that supports everyone, not just the handful of folks who are able to be paid to do the work." He continues, "It doesn't mean that people shouldn't work for social justice nonprofits, but if that's the main model we have for building movements, it limits us."

Tyrone himself now lives on very little money each year—$17,119.16 in 2008, actually (he keeps an Excel spreadsheet with all of his expenses). He tries to make as many of his own meals as possible, with an intention to buy locally grown, organic produce from the co-op he helps run. He pays $275 a month in rent, always takes the bus when he comes to New York to visit Elspeth (his partner, the program coordinator at RG), and spends very little on clothing and entertainment. One manifestation of his political principles, in line with globalization experts like Naomi Klein (author of *No Logo* and *The Shock Doctrine*), is a commitment to conscious consumption. Tyrone makes a note of every single thing he buys.

He also recognizes that living cheaply, ironically, is also a privilege of sorts. Tyrone wrote on his blog:

> One great thing about giving away this money is that it's made me think hard about living within my means. When I decided to give away most of my trust fund, I realized that I was going to have to get my act together financially and stop living like an irresponsible rich kid who could get bailed out by my parents whenever I over-drafted my bank account. . . . Of course, having class privilege means I get to see living on a really small budget as an exciting project rather than a stressful necessity. Truly being poor is expensive, and having had good healthcare my whole life, never having to go into debt, not having to take financial care of my family, and a million other things make it easy for me to live cheaply.

Tyrone is also opposed to ambition of the careerist sort, so emphasized for young Americans in today's preprofessional college environment. In fact, the idea of being part of this book, of being recognized as unique or special in some way, was initially extremely off-putting to him. Tyrone spent much of our first meeting trying to convince me of all the other grassroots activists that I should choose rather than him. Like a lover playing hard to get, he only intrigued me more.

Tyrone is fired up now, talking about grassroots movements the world over. He jumps from the economist Milton Friedman to the Ford Foundation and neocolonialism in Latin America, to memoirs by clandestine radicals, to the problems with elite philanthropy—all in a matter of minutes. It's hard not to be intimidated by the depth of Tyrone's knowledge. Probably noticing that I'm beginning to look overwhelmed, he takes a deep breath and says, "I get really excited about this stuff. I was talking to Elspeth about this. . . . There are certain conversations that I'm interested in having, but I realize I should sort of start at step one."

It's the wisdom of an older, more patient Tyrone—one who realizes that not everyone is as steeped in movement histories and social change philosophies. I can imagine him early in his political awakening, operating on six cylinders of new learning and outrage, unintentionally steamrolling less informed people. "Bottom line," he says, getting back to basics, "is that grassroots movements have always come from poor people, from disenfranchised people. They don't come from academics and philanthropists. Someone commented on Enough after foundations started losing all this money in the stock market crash, asking how horrifying it is that our movement funders are literally more invested in the success of capitalism than they are in the success of grassroots movements."

I want to believe—truth be told, I *have* to believe—that people sometimes do nothing to end suffering, or in the case of so much elite philanthropy, do inadequate or misguided things to end suffering, because they don't know another way. It's not that people don't care, that the rich who give copious amounts of money to the opera or the ballet have stones for hearts. It's not that they are superfans of free-market capitalism. (Okay, maybe some of them are, but they're rarely the ones dishing out lots of money to support the arts.) More often, it's that they have been socialized in a system where that is what people do with their money. They get psychological rewards—the beauty of the music, the recognition from their friends, the continuation of a family tradition. Most wealthy people simply haven't been inspired to see another way—as Tyrone, blessed with a very rebellious, curious nature, has—or had a powerful experience of a different kind of giving.

David Gilbert himself said, "In learning from history, we need to break from the mainstream culture that defines people as either purely 'good guys' or purely 'bad guys,' which can lead to the self-delusion that getting certain basics down guarantees that everything else we do is right. The WUO made giant errors along with trailblazing advances. Hopefully both are rich in lessons for a new generation of activists."

I can see Tyrone wrestling with this wisdom when he speaks about these issues, when he meets young people just being initiated into the community at RG and the idea that, in his words, "being rich is wrong." It takes such patience, such conscientiousness, a constant return to empathy despite all the forces that make it easier to see certain people as the enemy. And as it turns out, sometimes the easiest people to vilify are those who remind us most of ourselves.

Tyrone wrote beautifully about his own challenges with this on his blog after a recent conference:

In doing economic justice work with other class-privileged folks, I struggle with what often feels like a fine balance: trying to constantly betray and oppose the oppressive systems that I benefit from, while also having real compassion for myself and other folks who are struggling to find their way out of those systems in lots of different ways. Each year [at RG's national conference] we do an anonymous survey to collect data about how much money participants have and how much we're giving away, and then present the results in a slideshow during one of the plenary sessions. It's always shocking to see the results: millions and millions of dollars owned by the small group of people right there in the room (mostly inherited from wealthy families), and a minuscule percentage of it being given away. It's pretty disturbing to sit in such a major locus of massive wealth accumulation—

even more disturbing because we represent some of the very few rich people attempting to challenge economic injustice. It's an incredible illustration of how deeply the messages of capitalism—to hoard, protect, and grow wealthy—penetrate. I spoke with several anti-capitalist . . . attendees after the survey about our shared inclination to shout, "People—what are we doing!?? *We* are the problem!"

I try to remember that my rage against these systems is not objective or theoretical, but is a lot about how much I hate being in a role that often makes me complicit with massive global exploitation and oppression. I think my indignation and tendency towards ranting can be ways to push the pain of this away— like if I just constantly articulate some really well thought out critique of capitalism, and write things dissecting the ways that privilege functions, and drag all the privileged people I know into these really complex critical conversations, then I can distract myself from how much it all hurts and is sad.

Many of the young people who end up "coming out" at RG have passed as middle class their entire lives, mastering tricks to appear less wealthy than they are around new friends. Having their parents drop them off blocks before their destination so no one sees the Lexus, wearing thrift-store clothing, and complaining about imaginary debt are some perennial favorites.

The language—"coming out," "passing"—isn't just coincidental. One of the first things that I noticed, once I started hanging out with Tyrone and some of the other RG staff, is that the majority of them are queer, trans-identified, or both. Tyrone talks excitedly about how he came out at fourteen, at the same time as his own mother: "It was awesome!"

He didn't change his name to Tyrone or start asking that people use the masculine pronoun until his vagabond days. He describes coming of age in a queer community that was vibrantly redefining gender; he felt supported to claim the gender identity that felt most right for him, whether it was normative or not. Politically, his commitment to trans liberation is bound up in his commitment to broader economic justice; trans and gender-variant people are often the ones who are hardest hit by poverty, policing, and other forms of injustice.

Tyrone feels grateful today for the privilege of having had such a tight-knit queer community. "I don't always realize how nurturing it is until I step outside of it into a space where I'm the only queer or trans person," he says. "Now I work and organize a lot in spaces that aren't explicitly queer, but queer community was the air I breathed for a while, and I am so grateful for that."

So why the big crossover between the queer and radical giving communities? Tyrone ventures a theory about alienation: "If you're queer, you're more likely to have a negative experience of wealthy culture," he says. "That pushes you to critique the culture at large." Many of the kids who gravitate toward RG have been rejected by extended family members, harassed at school or on the streets, or experienced subtle judgment or a basic lack of understanding from parents and friends.

It makes a lot of sense. Wealthy people, children especially, tend to be insulated from the world of poverty. Tyrone explains, "Privileged people generally don't have to challenge ourselves. We're not the ones who are going to die. That's what inspires me about white antiracist organizing and groups like Resource Generation that are challenging the invisibilized role that capitalism and white supremacy play in injustice. That's what inspires me about solidarity movements of privileged people that make oppression our business and our responsibility. They're saying, 'We can't continue to live our lives in a bubble. We can see that there's a war against poor people and people of color, and that if we're not working for liberation we're a part of that oppression.'"

After wealthy queer kids experience discrimination, they're more likely to see it all around them. They may not declare war, like their predecessors in the sixties, but they certainly can't retreat back into their wealthy bunkers either.

TYRONE CLUTCHES A FAT MARKER in his hand and stands next to a big white flip chart. "When I first started coming up with my own giving plan," he says, "I wanted it to be perfect—politically speaking. I wanted to do the research and create this totally perfect thing that would redistribute my inherited wealth in the most socially just way, and then be done with it."

The ten young people seated in front of him in a U shape laugh a bit in relieved recognition. Guilt over the many complexities and hypocrisies inherent in being a left-leaning person with wealth is prevalent in this community. Karen Pittelman, whom Tyrone calls a "fabulous, radical philanthropist extraordinaire," gave away $4 million upon inheriting it at twenty-one years old. She also wrote a book—considered the primer on the movement—titled *Classified: How to Stop Hiding Your Privilege and Use It for Social Change*. In it she jokes, "Based on dedicated attempts by many of us involved with Resource Generation, we can say definitely that punching ourselves in the face does not resolve any of these contradictions."

One of the most interesting dynamics in the coming-out process for rich kids is rewriting some of the family mythology around how their wealth was earned in the first place. Many wealthy children are raised on very precious, and sometimes exaggerated, American Dream stories about the ways in which they came into wealth. These stories can mask the role of race and educational privilege, immigration status, exploitative practices (sweatshops, union busting), and other systemic factors that contribute to the process of wealth accumulation. Pittelman also writes, "Dealing with discrimination requires reclaiming individual identity. Understanding privilege, on the other hand, requires figuring out all the ways that we're not unique individuals."

Rich kids have to get sober about their family history, but also start to dissect their own lives in order to see the ways in which class privilege, not some special gift or mysterious divinity, has led to many of their opportunities. This is especially critical for privileged young people born in the eighties and nineties, many of whom were raised to believe they were rarified human beings destined for greatness, thanks to trends in affirmative parenting and self-esteem education run amuck. Many privileged children have actually been done a disservice by being pumped up on unrealistic expectations for their lives and shielded from the kinds of opportunities to fail and recover that create resilience.

Coming to terms with privilege is about not only rewriting family mythology but erasing family hubris. Many wealthy kids are raised to see their parents and other high earners or big inheritors as expert in a way the rest of the philistine world simply is not. In this worldview, it seems natural that rich people—who, again, *deserve* their excess wealth—are positioned to make the smartest decisions about how their donations might be spent to better humanity. The social justice philanthropy framework, in contrast, pushes privileged people to not only give away money, but also let go of a sense of superiority.

Tyrone has written the elements of this small but growing type of giving on the flip chart at the front of the room:

- Addresses root causes
- Inclusive decision making
- Makes the field of philanthropy more accessible and diverse
- Donors and foundations act as allies to social justice organizations and movements

"Social justice philanthropy grew out of the sixties and seventies liberation and community self-determination movements," Tyrone says in a patient, excited voice. "It's about actually changing systems, rather than providing Band-Aids."

One example that Tyrone often cites is a collaboration he engaged in with other RG-related young people, called Gulf South Allied Funders (GSAF). In the immediate aftermath of hurricanes Katrina and Rita, this small group of young people got together to brainstorm how they might leverage their own wealth, and the wealth of their networks, to get the people affected by the storms the resources they needed. They decided that they would give and raise one million dollars a year for three years to support grassroots rebuilding and social justice work in the Gulf Coast region—and rather than choosing whom to give the money to themselves, they would find a grant-making organization with strong ties in the region that could distribute the money to effective grassroots organizations.

Tyrone doesn't have as much access to old money as many of the other young people in RG. He didn't, however, use that as an excuse to avoid fund-raising from his extended network. "Despite the fact that my money hasn't been passed down for generations, I went to private school. I went to summer camp. We don't always admit that our socioeconomic circles include a lot of people with money, but if we're coming from a place of class privilege, they often do."

In March 2008, Tyrone brought his dad to New Orleans for a donor tour with the Twenty-first Century Foundation (the New York City–based black social justice foundation that GSAF partnered with). It was a moving experience for both of them. One night, after meeting with various grassroots leaders in rural Mississippi and Louisiana—mostly based in small local churches— Tyrone's dad turned to him and said, "This funding model makes so much sense—as an outside donor, you can't just look in the Yellow Pages under 'powerful community leader' and know who's doing this work. The relationship building [that Twenty-first Century is doing] is really important."

The next year, Tyrone returned to New Orleans for a month as a volunteer, working with grassroots groups like Safe Streets, Strong Communities, which is fighting police brutality and incarceration conditions in the New Orleans area—both huge problems post-Katrina. "What's happening in New Orleans in the aftermath of the storms is a really brutal example of the type of systemic violence that happens everywhere because of capitalism and white supremacy," Tyrone says. "Many of the people who have been doing the grassroots rebuilding work were fighting the same problems before Katrina. They're the problems poor people and people of color face everywhere—lack of affordable housing, lack of quality education, police violence, incarceration, racial profiling. . . . People started paying a lot of attention to these things after Katrina, but they aren't new."

The project Tyrone worked on had all the elements of social justice philanthropy. Rather than handpicking organizations worthy of their charity, as so many donors do, even in regions and fields they know next to nothing about, the Gulf South Allied Funders recognized what they did know—organizing rich people to support social justice—and what they didn't know— what folks in New Orleans needed and how they needed to get it. This approach requires humility and trust—two qualities rarely associated with the superrich.

AFTER THE WORKSHOP, Tyrone and I sit and catch up. His paternal grandmother has fallen sick, and Tyrone's dad and his dad's siblings had to relocate her to an assisted living home. The experience has shaken the whole family. "I think it tapped into some existential fear in my dad," Tyrone tells me. "He was really dealing with how much money it cost for my grandmother to have round-the-clock care. It brought up a lot of stuff about money and security and his desire for me to be okay and to be taken care of."

The experience prompted an intense conversation between Tyrone and his dad about the remaining money in his trust. Tyrone had planned on giving away his entire inheritance in a short period of time, and his dad had repeatedly urged him to reconsider. In previous conversations with his father, when Tyrone would talk about his projected giving plan, things sometimes devolved quickly. He says, "Eventually he would get scared and I would get indignant, and then he'd end up saying, 'You're young and idealistic.' And I'd say, 'You're a pawn of capitalism.' And the conversation would pretty much stop there."

But this time was markedly different. "We had a really deep interaction," Tyrone says. "For maybe the very first time, I really got that the money he'd set aside for me and my brother was so deeply based in love and wanting us to be taken care of. It doesn't change the fact that I don't believe in inheritance, but it's important for me to respect and appreciate that gift he gave me. People like my dad are particularly positioned to accumulate wealth with the help of a lot of race, class, and gender privilege, but of course it's also true that he worked really hard to support us. I'm trying to hold both pieces—the critique and the love."

When Tyrone thinks about planning for his future, he imagines investing in justice and community rather than in a big retirement fund. He wants to help build a world in which all people are taken care of, no matter how much or how little money they have. "The future's totally scary," he says. "Social Security doesn't take care of people, our resources are increasingly privatized, the U.S. is the only industrialized country without universal health care. . . . All you have to do is read an article about climate change to get totally freaked out about the future. But that's the psychology of capitalism, right? Make everyone feel so insecure that we hoard all the resources we can and forget how to share or take care of each other. I've noticed that often, the more money people have, the more scared and alone they feel. Real safety requires interdependence; wealth so often takes that away from us.

"We talked about how money doesn't make you safe, which, on one level, he agrees with. But on this other level, he just really needs me to hear him," Tyrone says. They talked about the possibility of Tyrone slowing down the process of giving away his trust fund. "I finally asked him, 'Dad, what are you going to be comfortable with?'"

Tyrone is compromising for now. He'll still give away half of the $400,000 in his trust fund by 2010, but the rest he agreed to leave untouched for a while, pending further conversation with his dad. He still plans to give most of it away, but he's willing to wait for a while and keep engaging his dad in the conversation. For him, it feels like maintaining a balance between his political ideals and the understanding that decisions like this are bound up in the complexity of human relationships and family.

"I think of giving money," he once wrote, "as one small facet of my social justice work that reflects my broader commitment to wealth redistribution, anti-oppression, and grassroots organizing." For now, he will continue his economic justice organizing and his food justice work with the Philly co-op. He gets excited about building bridges between radical philanthropists and the grassroots organizations that are leading liberation movements. He would like to continue to do workshops on radical giving and work toward creating an even more liberatory conception of social justice philanthropy. Tyrone would like to keep the WUO's intention, as described by Bill Ayers—"to show that 'the man' is penetrable"—alive and kicking in the twenty-first century.

Meanwhile, he will continue to wrestle with his own nature—the passion that leads him to inspired action but can also tempt him to fall into polarized thinking. Ultimately, what is most impressive about Tyrone Boucher is not his willingness to part with his trust fund—unusual as it is. Nor is it his intelligence or his penchant for adventure. What is most impressive about Tyrone is his courage to consistently examine himself. On his blog he writes:

> I've sometimes been encouraged by fellow organizers to take my political intensity down a notch because it can alienate people. It's important for me to hear this, because it reminds me how important it is to meet people where they're at, be compassionate and humble in my relationships with other radical or progressive folks who share my privilege, and work in my own communities to help build a strong multiracial, cross-class movement. I appreciate being challenged about this stuff, and it often serves as a much-needed check on my tendency towards stubborn indignation.
>
> But this conversation touches on something that I ponder a lot, something about militancy and ideology and the balance between being gentle enough to be accessible and having a political critique that is strong and uncompromising.

Reading Tyrone's words, I was reminded of Plato's old edict: "The unexamined life is not worth living." Suffering is hell. We must do everything we can to eradicate it. But in the meantime, we must also suffer the absolute terror of being honest about our own tendencies, our own gifts, our own limitations. We must see the ways in which we ourselves are the problem and—sometimes even more difficult—the ways in which everybody else, even the most unconscious of people, could be part of the solution.

Power Becomes Her

Rosario Dawson, actor and activist,
Los Angeles via New York City

Twenty-nine-year-old actor and activist Rosario Dawson is looking up at Jane Fonda with wide eyes, her mouth slightly ajar. Her eyelashes are thick and long as they reach toward the Eugene O'Neill Theater's ornate ceiling. She wrings her hands rhythmically in the dark, the long fingers of one hand tracing the inside of the other and then switching. She's truly mesmerized.

We've come to see 33 *Variations*, a play in which a musicologist (played by Fonda) dying of Lou Gehrig's disease researches why Beethoven spent his last years on earth composing variations to a mediocre waltz. Fonda's character is rigid, determined, and undeterred by her much softer, much more emotional daughter (played by Samantha Mathis). The core question of the play hangs in the air like a sort of existential smog: how does one blessed with unique gifts choose what to spend finite and precious life energy on?

When the house lights come up for intermission, Rosario and I stay in our purple velvet seats and talk about how stunning Jane Fonda's performance is. When Rosario joined the board of V-Day—Eve Ensler's antiviolence organization—in 2007, she began to get to know Jane, who is also on the board. I met Jane shortly thereafter, when she became my mentor through the

Women's Media Center, an organization she cofounded with feminist icons Gloria Steinem and Robin Morgan. When I told Jane about the book I was working on, she immediately recommended that I get in touch with Rosario, whom she described as "the real deal . . . truly doing radical work."

In addition to Rosario's active participation in the V-Day movement, she cofounded Voto Latino, a voter mobilization organization targeting the growing Latino American population, in 2004. In addition, she plays a large role, both financially and programmatically, in the Lower Eastside Girls Club. She's also, of course, an actor—having starred in a diverse range of movies, from *Explicit Ills,* an indy film about gentrification in Philadelphia, to *Seven Pounds,* a Hollywood blockbuster costarring Will Smith.

Rosario has a unique challenge, unlike any of the challenges faced by other activists profiled in this book—she has to reckon with an excess of power, not a lack of it. Endowed with celebrity status, she is constantly being approached, appealed to, sought out; her challenge is to distinguish her true passions, her true voice, her true activist identity from the cacophony of claims that surround her.

It might be easy for some stars to insulate themselves from injustice—the kind who revel in privacy, surround themselves with handlers, treat activism like a weekend chore for the rich and famous. Instead, Rosario has an exuberant, seemingly insatiable hunger for the world. She wants to live in the messiness of it. She is unguarded and multifaceted. As a result, she's forced to constantly face the vast discrepancy between the wealth and power she is afforded as a Hollywood figure and the lack of resources bestowed on the vast majority of others. Further, she exposes herself to those who are trying to attack this discrepancy on a daily basis—nonprofit executive directors, teachers, radical politicos—all of whom want to leverage her power for the cause. In other words, she's at the eye of the societal storm—weathering both the awesome responsibility that comes with her power and the wisdom born of her upbringing. She fights to keep one foot firmly planted in the "real world" in order to keep her power in perspective.

Rosario motions up at the empty stage. "I look at women like Jane [Fonda], like Eve [Ensler], like Rita Moreno, and I know they've got it figured out. They are everything at once. They teach me how to be an activist, an actor, an artist, a mother . . ." The lights dim, and she lets her list die on the vine as she turns with a huge smile back toward the stage.

ROSARIO MATERIALIZES ON A HAZY Los Angeles afternoon, striding down a broad sidewalk hugging L.A.'s Staples Center. She's wearing skinny jeans, knee-high boots, a blazer, and a smile—just as stunning in person as she is on screen. After giving me a warm hug, she lets the staff member at the door know that she's arrived—a fact that obviously brings great relief to the young woman charged with getting the celebrity speaker up to the reception as soon as possible.

The reception is a kickoff event for Peace Over Violence, a "campaign to raise awareness and educate the public about rape and sexual assault." Rosario has agreed to say a few words. The program is already underway in a lounge of sorts, so we slip in quietly and position ourselves off to the side. Though Rosario clearly doesn't want to disturb the event already underway, two successive staff members walk over and encourage her to come sit at the table for honored guests. Both times she sweetly refuses, saying that she's comfortable where she is. She kneels down, feeling a wave of panic wash over her.

Rosario isn't comfortable giving public speeches. She finds it far easier to embody someone else—even in front of a football team's worth of cast and crew—than to give a formal speech in front of a cocktail party's worth of people. She'd rather memorize someone else's words, convey someone else's ideas, than her own. It's not that she doesn't have plenty of both; a meal with Rosario is inevitably a mile-a-minute conversation about everything and anything, much of it carried by her. Rather, it's that she is still developing her sense of mastery around the issues that she cares about. "I resent the notion that celebrities are only there to perform," Rosario says, reflecting on her reticence to speak in public. "If I speak, I want to be studied, to really know my shit."

Soon she's ushered up to the stage, where she gives short remarks about the importance of ending violence all over the world, referencing the epidemic of rape in the Democratic Republic of the Congo—one of V-Day's target issues as of late. There's no trace of panic in her talk. "My passion for stopping violence against women was born while watching my own mom in action," Rosario explains to the rapt crowd. "She used to spend a lot of her time volunteering with a women's collective, and I learned so much from watching them all in action." When she finishes, the crowd of about 150 or so people clap enthusiastically. As I look around, I see the sort of titillation that people uniquely feel with a celebrity in close proximity, and I think how weird it must be to engender this kind of reaction. Rosario smiles as she makes her way back in my direction, seemingly unfazed.

After a politician, a couple of teenagers, and Sarah Tofte, an investigator from Human Rights Watch, also speak, the event winds to a close. Half a dozen people wander over to ask for a picture with Rosario or get her autograph. ("I love all of your movies!" "My girlfriend is going to flip when she sees this picture!")

Rosario entertains all of their requests with warmth, although she's actually eager to join Sarah Tofte and me. We're engrossed in conversation about a report Sarah has just authored on untested rape kits in L.A. County. I want to write a column about it. Rosario wants to explore the parallels between the work V-Day is doing to combat rape in the Congo and Sarah's more domestic, legalistic focus.

It is the first time, but it won't be the last, that Rosario will remind me of a reporter in her dogged pursuit of new information. She may be gifted at manifesting the imaginary, but her M.O. is all about fact-finding.

ROSARIO AND I ARE HAVING DINNER in Los Angeles, her newly adopted home. She's just flown in from New York, the home of her heart, the place that shaped so much of who she is and the work that she does in the world. On the plane, she read Malcolm Gladwell's new best seller, *Outliers,* which examines the key factors in exceptional people's success, essentially debunking the precious and very American notion of the entirely "self-made man." She tells me about it at a rapid clip: "The basic idea is that success comes through a combination of fate, hard work, and things like where you grew up and who influenced you."

"You must have really resonated with a lot of that," I suggest, thinking back over the magazine profiles I've read of her. "It seems like your life has almost every one of those elements."

"Right," she answers, nodding. "I mean, not the genius aspect, but definitely the combination of serendipity and hard work." Rosario is an irresistible blend of humble and secure—often referencing her work with great pride. It's not the pride of a celebrity who's been told she's great by a bevy of agents, publicists, and handlers, but the pride of an artist who has worked damn hard. Rosario has done thirty-eight films in her short career, rarely stopping to take a true vacation. Most of the time she's taken off has been devoted to her activism.

Gladwell writes, "It's not enough to ask what successful people are like. . . . It is only by asking where they are from that we can unravel the logic behind who succeeds and who doesn't." Rosario grew up on the Lower East Side in a squat during the eighties and nineties—a time of artistic richness and drug-addled poverty in pre-Giuliani New York. Her father, Greg, was a construction worker of European and Native Indian background. Her mother, Isabel, was a rebel of Afro-Cuban and Puerto Rican descent who loomed over Rosario's entire life, not in the sense that she was what we would today call a "helicopter parent," but in the sense that she was an unforgettable presence—both literally, at six feet tall with the huge, calloused hands of a plumber, and emotionally.

"She used to come pick me up from school with a weed leaf pendant dangling from a stud in her nose. It was incredibly distracting," Rosario says. "I'd be like, 'Come on, Ma, can't you just, like, put a ring in or something before you show up to sixth grade?'"

Growing up in a squat was an exhilarating experience for Rosario. Unlike the housing projects down the street, Rosario's building had no graffiti on it, and its residents rarely had to deal with violence or crime. The artists who lived there took great pride in their shared home. They siphoned off electricity from nearby streetlamps, broke bread together, and talked into the wee hours of the night. Rosario grew up bounding up and down between apartments—adored by all.

Isabel introduced Rosario to activism. Rosario remembers long afternoons spent cleaning out people's homes after they had died—an effort on behalf of Housing Works, a New York–based organization that fights AIDS and homelessness. "I can still feel the whole scene," Rosario says. "Looking at all the dead person's books, sweeping a sea of fleas off the floor, cleaning out the refrigerator, roaches lining the door." She starts laughing as her memory revs up. "I remember one time when I found a cock ring, and I asked my mom what it was. Of course, she told me straight up, even though I was, like, twelve."

The activism that Rosario's mom initiated her into was physical, connected to the community in which they lived and the people they loved (Rosario's uncle was HIV-positive), and done matter-of-factly. Helping out was not some sort of cross to bear or a college résumé builder.

In fact, the only time Rosario speaks regretfully about her childhood is when she talks about college; her parents didn't stress it, even though she was already taking calculus classes at Cooper Union when she was in high school. She has still never been to college. In its stead, Rosario is a voracious reader and learner and has an unusual capacity for recall. I've seen her instantaneously expound on everything from purity balls to flamingos, green building to *Battlestar Galactica*.

She also never attended college because destiny—in the form of controversial director Larry Clark and writer Harmony Korine—stepped in. They discovered fifteen-year-old Rosario—leggy, laughing, unstylish—sitting on her stoop one day and decided that she would be the perfect Ruby for their soon-to-be cult classic, *Kids*. Even though Rosario had no acting training and had never been drunk or had sex, she managed a completely natural performance as an experimental, out-of-control teenage rebel.

Gladwell writes that success "is not exceptional or mysterious. It is grounded in a web of advantages and inheritances, some deserved, some not, some earned, some just plain lucky." If Rosario hadn't lived in New York, where Clark and Korine were trolling for fresh, young faces and stoop culture is alive and well, she would never have been discovered. But if she hadn't been fearless—a quality gifted to her by her mother—or preternaturally gifted at acting, her luck would have added up to one bit part. Instead, it led to a life of challenging roles—on and off screen.

"I IDENTIFY FIRST AND FOREMOST with being a human, then with being a woman, then with being a New Yorker, and then being Latina," Rosario says. "It's never been my primary identity. I don't even speak Spanish, which sometimes makes it difficult."

She's explaining the unlikely beginnings of Voto Latino, the nonprofit organization that she cofounded in 2004 to increase American Latino youth civic participation. Unlike most organizations of its kind, Voto Latino doesn't have a genesis story mired in false starts, years and years of fund-raising challenges, or a leader with rabid determination. It has Rosario, who thought it was silly that the "Vote or Die!" campaign was mainly focused on P. Diddy's persona and even featured some celebrities in its PSAs who didn't, in fact, vote. She linked up with youth advocate Phil Colon, and together they started doing voter awareness work in the Latino community that just kept rolling into new opportunities until it eventually became an official organization.

According to a recent report from the Pew Research Center, the number of Hispanics in the United States will triple by 2050—representing nearly 30 percent of the total population. Much of this explosion in population is due to the immigration surge that began after 1965, when Congress abolished a quota system that had nearly ended immigration from non-European countries since the 1920s, and is intensified by the comparatively high birthrate among Hispanic Americans.

Latino youth, as a result, are a prime target for candidates interested in securing a voting base for the future. In the five battleground states (Colorado, New Mexico, Arizona, Nevada, Texas) where Voto Latino had the strongest presence in the 2008 election, Latino voter participation was at least five points higher than the national average. Voto Latino did good old-fashioned canvassing, but also employed its trademark Text2Represent campaign—the first national campaign of its kind—using cell phone texting technology to facilitate voter registration. Seventy-six percent of Latino youth who voted cast their ballot for Obama (Latinos, at large, voted for Obama-Biden two to one over McCain-Palin).

The demographic is complicated—influenced by a range of cultural and religious sources from Catholicism to Perez Hilton. As Keli Goff argues in *Party Crashing: How the Hip-Hop Generation Declared Political Independence*, no one should take the party affiliation of young people of color for granted anymore. Voto Latino is nonpartisan, so it doesn't push any one candidate over another, but Rosario—who registered voters herself on the streets of Denver during the Democratic National Convention—is a huge Obama fan. His biggest breakthrough with Latino voters came in Florida, where, according to the Pew Research Center, he won 57 percent of their votes in a state where Latinos have faithfully supported Republicans in the past.

"A lot of people figured we were just another one of those celebrity voting organizations that would ride in on a Hummer right around election time and then just disappear again after it was all over, but we had real staying power," Rosario says. Most of that is thanks to Maria Teresa Kumar, the cofounder and current executive director of Voto Latino, whom Rosario considers a close friend and "the heart and soul" of the organization.

Voto Latino is not just a voter registration entity; it's a cultural, political force trying to excite Latino youth about civic engagement year-round. It maintains a fairly active blog on all the issues of the day that Latino youth might care about, and it continues to hold events to promote politics, using the thirty-five-plus celebrities in its Artist Coalition to attract young people. Maria Teresa handles all of the day-to-day work, while also representing Voto Latino on MSNBC, NPR, the BBC, and CNN's *Anderson Cooper 360°*, among other international media outlets.

On occasion, Rosario will also appear on a television news show to speak about the importance of getting young Latinos involved in the political process. Rosario remembers one day when she agreed to do *Larry King Live* right in the middle of a really exhausting day of shooting the film *Eagle Eye*. "I was playing an agent of Air Force OSI, so I was already wearing a suit," she says. "That's something that I might have been really self-conscious about a few years ago—asking for thirty minutes in the middle of a shoot—but I'm okay with it now. And other people seem to be fine with it too."

Rosario actually took three months off from acting at the height of Voto Latino's work. She even left her grandmother, who was visiting from South Carolina, with her boyfriend while she attended the vice presidential debates. She laughs as she remembers the looks on both of their faces: "It's not like I've always been this super-political person, but I really believed in the moment, you know? I felt like I was building something important," she says.

Rosario wanted to be part of making history. Once, while we were talking about the prospect of each having children of our own, Rosario explained, "I want to have kids. I used to worry that I wouldn't have anything to teach them—anything of substance—but when I'm doing my activism, I feel like it's something I will one day be able to pass on to my children." It's an interesting sentiment for a woman with almost forty films to her credit at just thirty years old. But legacy isn't about fame for Rosario. It's about a meaningful, messy life; the high-profile film work is certainly part of it, but a much bigger part is the self-image she constructs offscreen.

WHEN ROSARIO TAKES THE STAGE to deliver the keynote speech for the Men Against Rape conference in Washington, D.C., she's a bit less nervous than usual. In this case, Eve Ensler, who was supposed to be there but had a scheduling conflict, has provided her with the speech. Rosario decides that rather than rewriting it in her own voice, she will basically channel Eve. In that way it will be more like acting than public speaking. "Just think short black hair and red lips," she tells the men. I imagine that few of the hundreds of men in attendance follow her instructions.

What might seem like a very awkward arrangement—Rosario using the first person while describing "my lover," "my son," and so on—actually makes a lot of sense. Ever since Rosario met her, Eve has been a close friend and mentor. Eve initiated Rosario into the V-Day organization, which has a very particular worldview and approach to activism—all shaped by Eve's persona. Women are warriors. Men are wounded. And everyone must band together by shouting these truths from rooftops, stages, and recently the Superdome in New Orleans—which the V-Day community reclaimed in a massive festival of performances, workshops, and celebrations in 2008. V-Day has contributed to everything from creating safe houses in Kenya and Haiti to helping motivate the Japanese government to issue an official apology to "comfort women" (women bound into military sexual slavery between 1932 and 1945), and from protesting continuing apathy in the face of femicide in Juarez to registering voters. Arguably its biggest impact to date has been on American college students; between February 1 and April 30 each year, college theaters across the nation are taken over by gangs of young women, giddy to stage the randy and intense *Vagina Monologues* (and Eve's subsequent plays).

Rosario was first initiated into "V-World"—and it is an entire world, complete with hand gestures, special language, and signature black and pink on everything—while starring in a production of *The Vagina Monologues* at the Apollo in 2006. Eve and Rosario—both fearless and fast talking, interested in looking at the toughest realities of human, especially female, existence—hit it off instantly.

In 2007 Rosario starred in and produced *Descent*, a low-budget, critically acclaimed movie in which her character avenges her own sexual assault by raping the rapist. The *New York Times*

said that *Descent* dramatized "the experience and the psychological aftermath of rape with a vividness . . . never seen in an
American film" and called Rosario's performance "intricate,
imaginative . . . equals those of Robert De Niro in 'Taxi Driver'
and Hilary Swank in 'Boys Don't Cry.'" Rosario screened *Descent*
for Eve and a small group of other V-Day organizers. It was controversial. Rosario says, "It was what you might call a mixed reaction, but Eve told me that she admired my boldness."

Eve eventually asked Rosario to serve on the board of V-Day.
"It was all really organic," Rosario says. "Eve's and my relationship just continually evolved until it made perfect sense that I
would be on the V-Day board."

Though activism itself, especially oriented toward easing the
suffering of women and girls, is native to Rosario thanks to her
mom, board leadership is a new experience. Her celebrity status
has given her the opportunity to influence on a scale that her
mom, no matter how powerful, has never been afforded. But to
Rosario, the gift of celebrity is also a curse: "In many ways, my
mom can do what I can't. She can roll up her sleeves and get to
work without anyone ever questioning her authenticity. Half the
time I feel like I have something to prove. Sometimes it actually
makes me want to hold back from using my celebrity. I have to
remember that it is part of my wealth."

In a culture that worships celebrity so fanatically, being a
celebrity can be dehumanizing. Rosario, like any activist, craves
to be part of communities working toward justice. Activism is
very rarely, if ever, a solo adventure. Rosario must cope with the
expectations, projections, and cynicism of others. Her power is
heightened, but so is the distance—however artificial—between
herself and those she works with and for.

One way that she seems to have learned to shrink that distance is with humor. It disarms people and reminds them that
she is just human, after all. Near the end of her speech, Rosario

goes off-script: "I might get in trouble for saying this, but I think we have a pretty vagina-friendly administration in the White House right now, don't you?"

The crowd erupts in laughter and applause.

THOSE CLOSEST TO ROSARIO expect this kind of unabashed, straight-from-the-gut talk from her. For example, Maria Teresa and Rosario accepted an award from the White House Project for their Voto Latino work on March 30, 2009, at UN headquarters in New York City. It was a fancy affair featuring hundreds of the country's most prominent female leaders, hosted by Soledad O'Brien. Geena Davis, who starred as the first female president in the short-lived TV show *Commander in Chief*, presented the award. As they were walking off the stage, Rosario leaned over to Geena—whom she had never met before—and said, "I love you so much. I'm trying not to dry hump you right now." Geena laughed so loud that people stared.

That's just how it is with Rosario—all excitement and no filter. She doesn't communicate through publicists or handlers. She's immediate and open. *Rolling Stone* editor Abbey Goodman became close friends with Rosario after interviewing her back in 1998. She reflects, "Rosario is more open to new experiences, new ideas, new people, and just absorbing all of it than I ever have been, and [unlike Rosario] I don't have strangers who think they know me or want something from me butting into my life on a near-constant basis."

But Rosario isn't a pushover, Abbey is quick to clarify. "She always filters those new experiences/people/ideas through her own value system. She isn't a sponge who just takes on other people's interests. She is open to expanding her horizons and never loses herself in the process."

I am also amazed at how Rosario seems to move through the world—a world that so often objectifies her—as a true subject.

She doesn't let her fame interfere with her humanity. After one meeting, we walked through the absolute center of Times Square on a Friday evening. Tourists shuffled along, often doing double takes at the sight of Rosario. A couple of guys on a corner cat-called the two of us—"Hey ladies, how you doin'?" (This is the kind of question I often answer with a grimace.)

"Great, thanks," Rosario replied graciously, with a big, genuine smile.

The guys recognized her then and exclaimed, "Oh shit! It's you!" She just sauntered by, laughing to herself.

About Rosario's openness, Abbey adds, "I've never seen her be mean to a fan or a car driver or a waiter or a fellow actor, even if she wants nothing more than to be left alone. Yes, she has natural social grace and a professional ability to mask hostility, but it always seems like something beyond that—that she's never truly bothered to her core, because she values human connection and interaction."

ROSARIO MOVES HER CAPPUCCINO out of the way, rubs her hands together in excitement, brushes her long, wavy hair out of her eyes, and leans over to get a better look at the blueprints spread before her.

It's brunch time on a Friday at the Grey Dog coffeehouse near Union Square in New York City. Rosario has just finished shooting a Chris Columbus teen action film in which the mythological Olympic gods are real and squabbling in the twenty-first century. Rosario plays Persephone, wife of Hades, stuck in the underworld, aka Los Angeles. It's an apt role for her, as Persephone was also discovered at a young age and torn from the protective embrace of her mother (Demeter) and thrust into a world of danger and seduction. What could be a better metaphor for the Hollywood that Rosario was initiated into at a very young age?

Now she's stopping in Manhattan on her way to Italy, where

she will be presenting the award for best actress at the Ischia Global Film and Music Fest (an honor she received the year prior for her role in *Seven Pounds*). She's packing in as many meetings as possible during the twenty-four hours or so that she's in town. Sarah Tofte (the Human Rights Watch investigator), myself, and Adriana Pezzulli-Newman, director of philanthropy at the Lower Eastside Girls Club, all sit in the corner of the coffeehouse with her, munching on french fries and talking about the Lower Eastside Girls Club's plans for a new library and leadership center.

"This is where the circular staircase is going to go up," Adriana points out, "leading into this reading space, where we're going to have a full library. This is where the book arts room is going to be. Girls will be able to use an old-fashioned printing press and make their own books."

"That is so exciting!" Rosario exclaims, eyes alight. "That is so radical! I learned all about that stuff for my role in *Seven Pounds*. It is so amazing! It's so important for the girls to be exposed to all of these different jobs they could do."

Adriana nods and continues to highlight different parts of the new center, ten years in the making. It's a truly dynamic space— mixing the old (the printing press) with the new (a new-media center), the local (a Lower East Side archive) with the global (an interactive map of the world). It's fun to watch Rosario take it all in and to imagine how much she would have enjoyed a space like this as an eager little girl on the Lower East Side. Her mom exposed her to a sort of urban potpourri of opportunities, but it probably would have been thrilling to have a real space of her own.

The Lower Eastside Girls Club, in fact, was created right after Rosario was discovered and her world had expanded far beyond her childhood neighborhood. According to their Web site, "By 1990 the Lower East Side had become the last neighborhood in the United States with the 'boys only' Boys Club distinction. A diverse group of Lower East Side women consisting of mothers, workers, artists, educators, scientists, athletes, business women and community activists organized in 1996 to address this obvious inequity." The Girls Club facilitates a range of activities in ethical, entrepreneurial, and environmental leadership for area girls—most of them coming from low-income minority families.

Rosario has agreed to host a fund-raiser to help the massive capital campaign that's underway to build the new site, and she and Adriana quickly discuss the best timing for that. "We're breaking ground in October," Adriana says, "so it would be great to do it sometime after that."

"Perfect," says Rosario. "I have this woman who I think would just love this whole thing, and I'm going to ask her to host." They speak at a rapid pace, as if time is running out. I imagine that Adriana often feels like that with Rosario, who is, in fact, heading off to JFK in a matter of minutes. When Rosario is present, she's really present, but she's also not easy to pin down. There are times when she looks at a script, takes a job, and is off shooting in a matter of weeks. She comes through New York often, but has family (her dad and brother still live in the city), business, and activism to balance while she's in town.

"I've been thinking about the board situation," Rosario goes on, "and I've decided that I can't do it. Since I've been on the V-Day board, I've learned a lot about how much work it takes. I don't want to weigh you all down with a slacker board member." Adriana and Rosario had been entertaining the possibility of Rosario joining the official board for months.

"Totally understand," Adriana says, nodding her head emphatically. "We'll put you on the board of visionaries—that's more fun anyway."

The necessary balance to Rosario's spontaneous, open personality is her aim to be accountable. She says, "My whole life so far I've been kind of like"—looking at an imaginary watch on her wrist—"'Huh, looks like I've got time. I'll try it.' Now I'm learning to say no." At thirty, Rosario has been making films for fifteen years. She's accepted roles as they've come, learned a lot from the amazing directors and activists she's had the fortune of working with, gone skydiving, run with the bulls. She's packed in the adventures; now it's time for the wisdom.

Adriana leaves, and Sarah, Rosario, and I hang around for a little longer. Sarah's partner is due to give birth to their baby at any moment, and we all reel with the excitement of it. Rosario talks about her goddaughter, and I talk about mine. Sarah gives us an update on the situation with the untested rape kits in L.A. County (more depressing news) and tells us a bit about her next research project on women veterans and sexual assault (I tell her about the women of SWAN). Rosario tells us more about the women's leadership center that V-Day is building in the Democratic Republic of the Congo. I talk about my book. We feel young and exuberant and full of conviction.

Reflecting on the day, Rosario later wrote: "Today was inspiring. I really like and admire the women we are. Every once in a while it's important to 'preach to the choir' and reinvigorate and reinforce the conversation. Differing and complementary as our approaches are, they make up the structure of a very real and young world that is tremendously conscious and global. I like to recognize it and I definitely want to live in it."

THE PLAY IS COMING to an end, and Rosario is staring up at the stage, still mesmerized. Kaufman's 33 *Variations* is about death and inspiration, and like any good play, it is also about what really matters in life—a sense of purpose, coupled with connection and love.

At one point during 33 *Variations*, Beethoven—supposedly going a bit mad from the desire to create and the unavoidable truth that time is running out—screams, "I am an instrument of God!"

It seems the perfect metaphor for Rosario. Since she was discovered on that stoop at Thirteenth and B in 1994, she has served as a vessel for so many people's words, outrage, artistry. She has been Larry Clark's promiscuous teenager, hungry for the world (*Kids*). She has been Spike Lee's post–9/11 vision of loyalty and loss (*25th Hour*). She has been Quentin Tarantino's final boot in the face of a stuntman stalker (*Grindhouse*). She has been Frank Miller's bloodthirsty, authoritative prostitute, manifest in a black and white and red tableau (*Sin City*). She has been the late eighties, AIDS-ravaged New Yorker walking into "warm, white light" (*Rent*), the hot, disgusted girlfriend in a sea of slackers (*Clerks II*), a gracefully dying graphic designer (*Seven Pounds*), a mother grieving with visceral, ugly pain (*Explicit Ills*).

Even in her activism, she has been an instrument—motivating and representing a new, more complex Latino political identity; channeling the depth and rage of Eve Ensler to end global violence against women; building a room of one's own for the girls on the Lower East Side.

It's not that she's a chameleon or confused. It's that she contains all of these multitudes. Like Jane Fonda before her, she will make mistakes. She will live many lifetimes. She will wear her celebrity like a snug coat—something that fits her beautifully, but can be taken off when unnecessary. She will make great art and maybe a little bad. She will have strong opinions and say them aloud. And she will have a damn good time leaving her mark on a world still not used to stunning, raw, unapologetic women.

When the curtain falls, Rosario turns to me with childlike exuberance and gives me a big hug. "Wasn't it amazing?" she asks, eyes still wide.

Born to Teach

Dena Simmons, eighth grade teacher, Bronx, New York

The eighth graders jostle into the room, all inside jokes and graphic sweatshirts, their headphones hanging out of their pockets, their Nikes improbably clean. When they see the spread—grapes, celery, carrots, apples, peanut butter, cheese, crackers, and brownies, all bought by Miss Simmons—and hear the jazz music leaking from an old boom box, they start buzzing with excitement.

Twenty-six-year-old Dena Simmons doesn't look like she would demand such authority, but when she stands at the front of the room, the students slip into their desks and quiet down, all eyes on her. Her light skin matches the hue of most of the Latino teenagers in the room, though she is actually half West Indian—her mother immigrated to the United States from Antigua—and half Russian Jew. Standing at five feet even, dressed in a white button-up shirt and black pants, her jet-black hair pulled back into a bun, she begins: "Welcome to Classroom 823's coffeehouse."

A few of the girls in the front row reply with a mockingly formal, "Why, thank you," and giggle in one another's direction.

Dena continues, "I just want to remind you that we are a family, a community. There is no reason to be scared. If someone shares something personal, consider it a privilege. You are all very good at this already."

Darien (all names of children in the class have been changed to protect their privacy), a spindly black kid, already almost six feet tall at just thirteen years old, is folded into a desk in the last row, sucking the thumb of one hand, while the other grips the sheet of paper he found on his desk listing the order in which the students will read their narrative essays aloud. He looks worried.

All you can see of Chris, the kid next to him, is his bald head shining in the sunlight. He's got his face down in his arms, which are folded on his desk.

"I'm not taking any requests for changes in the order," Dena says. "This is good practice. When you all go to college, you'll have to present." Suddenly a childlike smile melts the authority right off her face as she exclaims, "I'm very excited!" She heads to the back of the room and slips into an empty desk as the first student nervously approaches the front of the room, where a sign taped to a file cabinet reads: "YOU'RE AMAZING! MS. SIMMONS ♥ YOU."

Hema is a beautiful combination of cultures—East Indian ancestry, first-generation American with parents born and raised in the West Indies, and a definitive Bronx accent. Her long black bangs obscure her left eye as she tentatively reads an essay about discovering that her parents had left two siblings, an older brother and a sister, behind with her grandmother in Trinidad.

Next is Deasia, an already tiny girl who looks even tinier in her skinny black jeans. She talks about her mother and father, whose relationship has been "like a dramatic, romantic movie." She seems to revel in the performance, explaining how her mother never gave up on her father while he was in jail. Wrongfully accused, of course.

And then there's John, a boy with long curly hair and a black hoodie with a white skull airbrushed on it, who describes being discriminated against by a clerk at Macy's. He reads quickly, clearly unaccustomed to being the center of attention.

Student after student, they rise from their desks, stand at the front of the room, and share personal stories filled with image-rich metaphors and visceral emotion (Dena has gone through two, and sometimes three, revisions with each of them). At twelve and thirteen, their struggles are mostly about identity, family, and alienation.

All of them have been touched by immigration issues, and a majority are new immigrants themselves—mostly from the Dominican Republic, Puerto Rico, the West Indies, or Africa. They reveal rich fantasy lives about responding to unkindness, and an unmistakable resentment toward their parents—who star as unreliable, always moving, deeply distracted characters in their personal dramas. America—a harsh, overwhelming land—is the setting. Excerpts from three different essays:

"Every day, I watched my mother pamper that baby the way she never pampered me. I hated her for every breath she drew from her nostrils."

"I was only ten when I first came to the U.S. with my mom, sister, and little brother. Everything was different to me. It was as if I was a little mouse in a world of giants."

"Whatever you do, just remember, I ain't white."

And one student reads a deadpan summary of love's power, which could also be interpreted as an apt description of Dena Simmons's philosophy of teaching:

"Everyone says love is a big word. One way it works is to make everything better than before."

Dena teaches eighth grade at the Urban Science Academy, a middle school that occupies the third floor of a drab brick building at 1000 Teller Avenue in the heart of the Bronx—the poorest urban congressional district in the country. The Urban Science Academy was created in 2004, when a larger, and largely failing, middle school was divided into three—the latest trend in urban educational reform. There are now 475 fifth through eighth grade students at the school, 25 of them seated in disciplined rows in Classroom 823.

Dena knows her students extremely well, having taught them for three years in a row. This isn't customary at the Urban Science Academy, but Dena requested the opportunity to stick with her students so she could really invest in them over a period of years. When asked whether accommodating the request was disruptive to the rest of the school schedule, Principal Patrick Kelly says, "Traditional thinking about inner city education has resulted in generations of miserable failures. Dena is such a good teacher that I knew she could make it work. I'd put my own kid in her class."

In fact, Kelly has known Dena since she was just a kid, having been the assistant principal at her private Catholic elementary school, also in the Bronx. "She's massively intelligent, very passionate about overcoming racial, social, and economic barriers," Kelly says. "She is a living embodiment for these kids of where resilience, strength, and determination can get you."

Indeed, Dena is the kind of person whose résumé not only impresses but exhausts you. In 2004 she received the highly competitive Truman Scholarship, $26,000 in graduate school funding for which there are usually six hundred nominees and sixty winners. She graduated magna cum laude from Middlebury College in 2005. She went on to Santo Domingo on a Fulbright grant, where she studied teen pregnancy, eventually presenting her findings to the first lady of the Dominican Republic.

In 2006 she returned to the Bronx, her home, as a Teach for America corps member, teaching sixth grade at the Urban Science Academy while pursuing her master's degree in childhood education at Pace University in the evenings. She spent the summer of 2007 in Antigua, studying the sexual and reproductive health of sex workers as an unpaid intern of the national government. In 2008 she graduated summa cum laude and spent the following summer, once again unpaid, translating critical documents about maternal and child health into Spanish for an international health organization.

Even so, what is most impressive about Dena is not featured on her résumé. She has an instinct for creating a classroom culture that makes teenagers from some of this country's poorest, most maligned circumstances feel a profound sense of dignity.

In fact, Miss Simmons's class exists in an alternate reality. In a district where (according to Gotham Schools, an independent news source about the New York City public schools) the graduation rate was 40 to 49 percent in 2008, every one of her students believes he or she will not only graduate high school, but go to college. Their classroom blog, in fact, is headlined "College Bound: 1 teacher. 25 students. All from the Bronx. Ready to show the world what we are made of."

In a culture where too many of her students have already been exposed to or experienced violence, Dena's classroom is a sanctuary of gentleness. "We can't control the world out there," she often tells her students, "but in here, it's all peace and love." She points to the two giant banners near her cluttered metal desk that, indeed, read PEACE and LOVE. Throughout the day, it's not unusual to hear one of Dena's students, female or male, casually say to her, "I love you, Miss Simmons," and to hear her respond, "Love you too," as if it is the most natural thing in the world.

And in a borough where, according to the federal government, the median household income is $28,173 and 28.2 percent of folks live below the poverty line, Dena says, "This classroom is a private school as far as I'm concerned." She takes her students on frequent field trips—to Wall Street, to museums, to the New York Film Festival, and, most exciting, to Middlebury College in Vermont. The trip to Middlebury at the end of the year is held up as the shining reward for months of dedicated work—a time when Dena will show the students what college is like as they get a twenty-four-hour break from the city grit and family drama.

Dena raises the money to hire a bus and feed the students all on her own. "I want them to really experience the campus and feel like they belong there," she says.

I ARRIVE AT THE URBAN SCIENCE ACADEMY on a Friday at 5:00 a.m., exhausted and dressed in an old sweatshirt and sneakers, my backpack slung over my shoulder. We have a long bus ride ahead—five and a half hours to Middlebury. As I approach the school, still awash in darkness and a light drizzle, I am shocked at the scene: eighteen middle school kids, standing in small groups and chatting with birthday-like excitement, dressed in their Sunday best. "They've been here since four thirty," Dena says, greeting me with a smile and a hug.

The girls have interpreted Miss Simmons's directions to "make a good first impression by looking nice" in various ways: everything from silk dresses to trendy shirts with high-waisted belts, purchased on sale from Conway. Everything is tight, cinched, sucked in. A few of the girls hobble around in uncomfortable shoes, their legs bowed from the pain.

The boys' transformation is especially striking. They have gone from the characteristic cloak of hoodies and baggy jeans—so much material to hide their awkward bodies within—to ill-fitting suits, painstakingly pressed by their mothers the night before. Their button-ups and ties clash with competing patterns. Somehow these ensembles make them seem more vulnerable, terrifically young. Darien is dressed in a black suit, the pant legs a couple of inches shy of his ankles. John has his bushy hair pulled back in a smooth ponytail and wears an electric-blue button-down shirt, a thick navy tie, and black dress pants. Chris is the only one not wearing a suit; his baggy jeans still hang off his tiny frame, the collar of his fuchsia and blue shirt the only gesture toward formality.

When the bus pulls up, everyone piles in, and I'm again surprised that there's no controversy over who sits where and with whom. The only one left alone is Chris, who immediately puts his gray sweatshirt on the window and leans. A group of students discuss whether this is okay, but when Chris assures them that he doesn't mind having a seat to himself, they settle in. As soon as all the kids have slid into place, they discuss which DVD to watch, out of the many that the driver has piled in a plastic bag. They choose *Rent*. I smile to myself and think of Rosario.

DENA SITS WITH THE HEAVY ENVELOPE in her lap for a few moments before opening it. Of course she's been the recipient of plenty of heavy envelopes over the years, but this one feels particularly weighty. It carries the promise of reaching the highest educational level possible at the most prestigious university in her field—a true pinnacle.

Most of the best and brightest teachers are eventually lured away by intellectual curiosity, higher salaries, leadership aspirations, burnout, or a combination of these forces. Turnover, in fact, is one of New York schools' most pernicious problems. Principal Kelly assures me, when I speak to him in April, that he'll be retaining forty-two out of forty-five teachers for the 2009–2010 school year—a new record for the Urban Science Academy. (In fact, he will lose twelve.)

He doesn't know about Dena's heavy envelope and the promise inside: she has been accepted into an EdD program at Teachers College, Columbia University. It's in the Department of Health and Behavior Studies, the equivalent of a PhD in health education.

She's torn about whether to go, even entertaining the possibility that she might pursue her doctorate part-time and still teach full-time, but she's also worried that going part-time would affect her financial aid. She can't imagine leaving the school, leaving the classroom, leaving her kids. But there's another part of her that wants to step back.

"Does going to grad school feel like selling out somehow?" I ask.

Dena's face changes. I think it's a look of irritation, something I've never seen from her before. "Selling out?"

I immediately regret my word choice and stumble around in my attempt to clarify. "I mean, if the most immediately important work you can do is in the classroom affecting kids' lives, then even though the long-term effects of your EdD could be great . . . . I don't know . . . Teacher retention, especially great teacher retention, is such a problem."

"It seems like people only use the phrase 'selling out' when talking to people of color," Dena says, her face still tense. "I spend a lot of time taking care of other people. I put myself on the bottom of the list. This could be a chance to do something for me, to learn something that I can hopefully bring back to the Bronx. I'm not going to burn any bridges. I'm going to stay connected to the school."

I hit a nerve—not just, it seems, because of the racial implications of my word choice, but because Dena really is struggling to feel okay about wanting to do something for herself. It's clear that her dilemma feels like Sophie's choice—leave the kids and get a prestigious degree and a bigger perspective on their suffering, or stay with them and heal them on a daily basis but continue to operate in a system that is horribly broken. She looks out the window and says, "It's going to be a really hard decision."

HARD DECISIONS ARE A NEW LUXURY in Dena's family, where basic survival has not always come easy. When she tells the story of her mother, you feel as if you are hearing an uncensored version of Cinderella. Jacklyn, Dena's mother, was born to a neglectful mother in Antigua in 1950. She was soon dropped off at her father's home, where she was forced to endure the wrath of a stepmother who resented her presence (she was essentially a mistress's mistake) and made it known by feeding her the leftovers from the dinner table, if at all. When she wasn't fed, she would try to grab scraps out of the pigpen in her father's yard. She was asked to go to the back of the house when guests came over.

When white folks—usually vacationing, or stationed on a U.S. military base located on the island—dropped off clothing donations at the house, her stepmother would actually let Jacklyn try on the dresses, comment on how pretty she looked, and then turn them all into bags and dust rags so she couldn't enjoy them. Instead she made Jacklyn dresses out of harsh material that itched. When Jacklyn would fidget under the scratchy material while sitting in church, her stepmother would shake her head and say, "No class," under her breath.

When Jacklyn was just five years old, one of her girl cousins told her that another cousin, this one male and seventeen, wanted to play with her under the porch. Thrilled to finally be included, she went happily, only to discover that she had walked into a trap. She was raped. Not for the last time. Her half brothers would repeatedly sexually assault her over the years.

The only shining light in Jacklyn's adolescence was a teacher who gave her the one-on-one attention that she was so starved for and told her that she was worth a damn. Jacklyn held this teacher's words inside her head, a secret weapon against total annihilation in a family that was doing everything it could to destroy her. The words even gave her the strength to start befriending some of the white people who lived nearby. Eventually one of the families would sponsor her to come to America.

It was 1969, and the Bronx Concourse may have been one of the poorest spots in America, but it felt like heaven to Jacklyn. She found a job managing the maintenance of a few local buildings. She was good at it; making sure people had their needs met—heat, water, safety—felt like sweet revenge after years of never having her own needs heeded.

Eventually she would start dating a Russian Jew who owned a furniture store. He was twenty years her senior but treated her kindly—an experience she'd never had with a man. At thirty-one she had her first child, Shana, and at thirty-three she bore twin girls—Dana and Dena. The Russian fled the scene, and Jacklyn figured it was just as well. She would create her own little haven of girls. Their one-bedroom apartment was small, but their dreams would be big. She would see to it.

The little family of women lived in a one-bedroom apartment for most of the girls' childhoods. Dena says, "At night the sounds of gunshots kept me awake, and Dana and I, who slept in the same full-size bed, clenched onto each other, shivering, trying our best not to move." Even so, Dena wouldn't choose to have grown up anywhere else: "I loved being surrounded by so many people from so many different places. I loved the resilience and flavor that people in the Bronx have."

By eighth grade, Dana developed a mysterious and debilitating ailment. She was throwing up constantly, nearly every day, no matter what she ate. Dena remembers hours and hours spent on the floors of crowded hospital lobbies, waiting so that her twin could see a doctor, who would inevitably shrug his shoulders, call it psychosomatic, and hustle the family out the door. It was on those waiting room floors that Dena's commitment to healing the public health system was born. She couldn't believe how her family, how her pained, writhing twin, was treated with such indignity.

Eventually they found a doctor who took long enough with Dana to give a diagnosis: cyclic vomiting syndrome, also called abdominal migraines. It is characterized by acute nausea and vomiting, usually between six and twelve times an hour. An episode can last from a few hours to well over three weeks. There is no known cure.

For Dana, of course, the pain was excruciating. For Dena, it was galvanizing. "I had such a sense of powerlessness watching my sister suffer. It made me want to do what I can, when I can. If there's a solution to be found, an action to be taken, I'm going to do it."

By middle school, Dena was already showing signs of being a natural teacher. In fact, the principal used to send her to lower grades, mostly first or second, when the regular teacher didn't show up, and she would substitute for the whole day. She reveled in having a rapt audience of little people. She was in charge. But when her mom caught wind of it, she called the principal and demanded that Dena spend her school days as a student, not a teacher.

Eventually the family was able to get Dana's symptoms under control enough that she headed off to Westover, an all-girls boarding high school in Connecticut, alongside Dena. Jacklyn had seen boarding schools on television and knew she wanted that kind of opportunity for her daughters; they had full-ride scholarships to the school, which currently costs $41,400 a year.

Dena was excited: "I wanted to leave so badly. I figured, what does the Bronx have to offer me?" But encountering boarding school culture—white, predominantly wealthy, cliquish—for the first time was jarring. "Right away I felt inferior," she says. "I figured I wouldn't have any friends. It was like they spoke a different language from me."

Her classmates found her exotic. "What is it like living in the Bronx?" they would ask, eyes wide, images of "the ghetto" they'd seen on television flashing through their minds. It was the first time Dena realized that she was a minority or that she was considered poor by the rest of the world. "Up until then," she says, "I figured I had enough of everything. I had food, because we had food stamps if we needed them. I had a home. The fact that it was a one-bedroom apartment didn't seem strange to me. Everyone in the Bronx was a person of color, so that always seemed perfectly normal to me too."

Resilient and adaptable, Dena eventually made close friends and adjusted to boarding school life. She threw herself into academics, even though she could never shake the feeling that all her peers were smarter than she was. "I didn't think I was good at anything," she says. "I was always really hard on myself." Even so, when Dena heard all the other girls talking about college, she decided she would like to go too.

Outside of academics, she had a lot on her mind. Eventually Dana's symptoms got so bad again that Jacklyn decided to move closer to her girls. The school offered her a job on staff as a weekend security guard. With Shana ten minutes away at Taft—another elite boarding school—it was like the family was back together again. Dana and Dena both thrived, and in the fall of 2001, Dena headed off to Middlebury College.

Today Shana is beginning her law practice after graduating from Berkeley Law in the spring of 2009. Dana was working in development at Western Connecticut State University, but lost her job—mostly because her sickness affected her reliability at work. Jacklyn still does a combination of security and administrative work at Westover, six to seven days a week.

Of their collective success, Dena says, "My mom is alive and in this country because she's a fighter. She instilled that in us— all of us are fighters. There's no other option."

BACK AT MIDDLEBURY, it's time for the admissions office talk. The eighth graders sit in two rows, keeping fidgeting to a minimum despite the fact that they've just spent five and a half hours on a bus. (Some napped, but everyone was woken up when Deasia spotted an alien-looking animal out the window and screamed, "What is that?!" It was a llama.)

The Emma Willard House of Admissions is pristine. The room that the kids sit in has white silk wallpaper with ornate, gold-framed drawings of birds and plants. The pink curtains draped in multiple layers on the big, clean windows match the thick pink carpet. The furniture is all antique—dark, old wood polished to a fine shine.

Bob Clagett, the dean of admissions, stands in front of a big white tablet on an easel and says, "I sign all the admissions letters."

"Did you sign Dena's?" one of the students immediately asks.

"I think Dena got in before my time, but you all should know that you are unbelievably lucky to have a teacher like her." The kids look over at her and beam. They already know.

Dean Clagett tells the students, "The point is not necessarily that you come to Middlebury. The point is to expose you to just one college. That's what it's all about—exposing yourself to new ideas."

The dean gives them a quick rundown of all the different kinds of colleges and universities in the U.S.—private versus public, rural versus urban, residential versus commuter. He talks to them about the virtues of a liberal arts education. He briefly mentions financial aid, avoiding the subject of tuition. (Middlebury's tuition is $50,400 a year, almost twice what most of these kids' parents make. Forty-three percent of Middlebury students are on financial aid, and the school has a need-blind admissions policy.) The dean asks, "Has anyone heard of Ann Landers?"

The kids stare back at him blankly, some shaking their heads no. Dean Clagett lets out a little giggle of enjoyment and says, "I didn't think you would. Well, she was an advice columnist, and she always said, and I'm paraphrasing, that success is that point where two lines cross." He draws one thick black line and says "Preparation," and then draws another line intersecting the first and says "Opportunity." The kids copy his diagram in the notebooks open on their laps. It all seems so simple.

Until Manuel Carballo, associate director of admissions and coordinator of multicultural recruitment, takes over. It's not that he's intimidating. In fact, quite the opposite—his round face and gentle manner are fit for children's television or family therapy. But the information he's giving the students suddenly seems to overwhelm them.

"What do you think is the most important thing for getting into a college like Middlebury?" he asks.

"Grades?" John, a nearly straight-A student, answers.

"Exactly. We are expecting a lot of As. A couple of Bs are okay, but we don't want to see students with any Cs. We put a big red circle around those." The students start to look at one another with nervous faces.

"What about the SATs?" one student asks.

"Don't worry about SAT scores," Manuel assures them, surprising me. "You can go online, take some practice tests." I think about all of their Manhattan peers who are already studying for the SAT with private tutors. According to the *New York Times,* a quarter of the students who take the SAT spend from four hundred dollars into the thousands on prep. Ann Landers's easy lines of preparation and opportunity are already looking less straight.

"How much do the SATs cost?" Deasia asks.

"It's about seventy-five to a hundred dollars these days," Manuel says. When they collectively gasp at the price tag, he quickly adds, "But many of you will qualify for a fee waiver." I'm struck that if the price of the SAT sounds outlandish, wait until they learn about the price of a college education.

"Your behavior is also important," Manuel goes on. "Your transcript will tell us how many tardies you've had."

"Parties?" Darien asks, coming alive from a half-awake state. Everyone laughs, but I can tell that he actually has no idea what tardies are. "Latenesses," I whisper in his ear.

Chris is curled onto himself, head in arms, not even looking in Manuel's direction. Another girl is sucking her thumb. A phone goes off, belting out Christina Aguilera's "Beautiful," and Dena gives the culprit a death stare. The rest of the kids start asking bizarrely specific questions:

"Okay, so let's say you're in high school, right? And you're confused in a class, right? So you ask your teacher questions, but she don't answer you. What do you do?"

"What happens if you fail gym?"

"So what if you're taking a language, like Spanish or whatever, and then you drop it?"

Manuel answers each of them patiently, emphasizing that failing any class is really out of the question if you want to get into a good college, and further, that the admissions counselors will be looking to see that you made the best of your situation, even if it wasn't ideal. He emphasizes that they are being introduced to college at a perfect moment, because they're starting with a blank slate heading into high school.

"The only person that can bring you down is yourself," Dena says. "The only person that can bring you up is yourself."

Manuel adds, "Every single door is open to every single one of you. I mean that." The students now look overwhelmed, as if the only door they want to go through is the one out of the admissions office.

MIDDLEBURY WAS DENA'S FIRST CHOICE, plain and simple. There were other schools that gave her a more generous financial aid package, but her mom assured her that money wasn't everything. Holding up a broken wine bottle opener, she said, "Dena, remember how I got this at the dollar store? It doesn't even work right. You pay for what you get."

Dena says, "She wanted me to see that even though I had to pay more to go to Middlebury, it was an investment. It would pay off in the end."

Even though Middlebury has a reputation for Birkenstocks and trust funds (it is the only college in the country with its own golf course *and* its own ski slope, nicknamed "Club Midd" by many students), Dena thrived there. For the first time in her life, she worried about her sister from afar instead of being constantly intertwined with her daily health struggles. (Dana went to Trinity in Hartford, Connecticut.) Dena read voraciously, got hyperinvolved in extracurricular activities—she even cofounded her own organization to teach local residents' children about diversity (the town is about 95 percent white)—and started on her path to become a teacher.

When Dena returns to the campus, it's not just students who light up when they see her, but professors and cafeteria workers and even the college president. Absolutely everyone seems to know her personally. After watching her walk around campus for a few hours, I start to understand that it was here that Dena first understood the importance of learning communities—a concept she stresses like a broken record in her classroom. She had deep relationships with her professors; she, in turn, creates these kinds of bonds with her students. The Middlebury community saw a lot in Dena Simmons, and today she sees that potential in Darien, John, Hema, and the others. Straining to meet high expectations, with the safety net of a present, loving teacher, is a circus act she motivates her students to perform every single day. Middlebury, Vermont—with its rolling green hills and fleece vests—couldn't be more different from the towering projects and puffy jackets of the Bronx, but the formula turns out to be highly replicable.

There's one crucial ingredient of Dena's breathtaking success as a teacher that wasn't learned at Middlebury and can't be replicated: her background. Just ask those who have done Teach for America.

FOUNDED IN 1990 by then Princeton undergrad Wendy Kopp, Teach for America (TFA) is one of the most popular postgraduation programs for America's young, elite, and altruistic. In 2009, according to Teach for America, there were 35,000 applicants for 4,000 spots. Over two-thirds of the 2009 corps is white.

Those lucky enough to get into the program commit to two years of teaching in some of the country's poorest schools, both urban and rural; in exchange, they are promised rigorous training, ongoing mentoring, and the opportunity to earn a graduate degree in education. The thinking behind the program—widely regarded as one of the most groundbreaking educational interventions in the last twenty years—is, as Kopp wrote in her memoir, *One Day, All Children,* that "if top recent college grads devoted two years to teaching in public schools, they could have a real impact on the lives of disadvantaged kids."

But as the over fourteen thousand people who have gone through the program over the last eighteen years have learned, being a top college grad doesn't always translate into the skills— or, more controversially, the identity—necessary to manage a classroom in a low-income school. According to a 2009 MSNBC report, most TFA teachers leave the profession after the required two years. Between 10 and 15 percent of each corps class drops out before finishing the program. I got a good glimpse of the reason one afternoon at the Urban Science Academy, when I peeked into another teacher's classroom.

I had spent the morning watching Dena's class work on the slope-intercept form; the students were mesmerized as Dena did a few equations on the board, and then they struggled through their initial confusion by teaching one another. Dena strikes a very interesting balance in her teaching style—preferring to be a sort of patient guide in the background when it comes to the actual subject material, but being deeply enmeshed with the students' emotional and social lives. When the learning clicked into place, the kids performed their joy—doing little happy dances and exclaiming, "Now I get it! It's mad easy!" and "Miss Simmons, math is all about common sense!"

In contrast, the mood in the random language arts class that I'd slipped into was pure resistance. The teacher was a young, fairly round white guy with a soft, bearded face, who looked like he was probably the heartthrob of the theater kids at his high school in some Midwestern town. He was anything but the heartthrob now, standing in front of the class of just seven students with an exasperated look on his face, trying to initiate a conversation about the themes in *Othello*: "Have you ever been jealous of a friend? Is jealousy wrong? Why or why not?" The students were supposed to be discussing in small groups, but instead they were involved in myriad distractions, and the teacher kept getting sidetracked by feeble attempts at discipline, mostly empty threats and frivolous rewards. One kid was burping, another sighing just loudly enough to drive the teacher crazy, and another went to the bathroom, never to return. The one girl in the class slept with her head down on the desk.

The teacher had prepared placards with the characters' names on them that the students could wear around their necks, but when everyone got in a fight over who got to wear which placard, he finally just turned down the lights and turned on the television. They spent the rest of the class period zoning out in front of *O*, the modern film version of *Othello* starring Julia Stiles and Mekhi Phifer.

I couldn't blame him. In the hour that I'd sat in his classroom, I'd grown bone tired. I felt as if I'd lived a week in those sixty minutes, watching him struggle for authority, seeing such ineffectiveness and apathy. Even *my* posture, I realized, was slumped.

There could be many things that separated Dena and this poor guy, but the one that seemed most obvious was that the students felt no obligation to respect him, no access to identify with him. He was just another well-intentioned white kid from a fancy school who thought he was going to "save them" by making *Othello* relevant. Instead they all flailed in their disconnect.

Though Dena is no longer in the TFA corps, she recounts a meeting during her second year of teaching when a young white woman looked at her, shocked, and said, "You're in Teach for America? I thought you were a real teacher."

"As opposed to a fake teacher?" Dena responded, giving her what she calls her "Dena-from-the-Bronx look." The woman just brushed it off.

"It's a costume they put on," Dena says to me of the TFA zeitgeist, shaking her head. Though Dena has infinite patience with her students, she appears to have very little for teachers who she believes "don't get it." I once observed her in a staff meeting in which the majority of the teachers—many of them from TFA—joked and chatted with one another, while Dena simply filled out the necessary paperwork and left.

It's not that white kids, or kids from privileged backgrounds, can't be great teachers in low-income schools. But the assumption that an Ivy League or elite liberal arts education prepares someone to be an effective teacher is a fallacy. Teaching is a complex art of performance, intellect, innate instinct, patience, cultural awareness, and courage—perhaps one of the most complex professions around. It's not a community-service pit stop on the way to a real career. It's one of the hardest and most influential jobs a person can hold. So if you're not cut out for it, if teaching isn't something you're deeply called to do—as it is for Dena—then the classroom can be torturous.

Add in the cultural factor: thousands of well-intentioned white kids, just like the one I observed, doing all the right things and getting all the wrong results. They're not bad people; they just aren't easy to identify with for a bunch of kids from Chicago's South Side or South Central L.A. or the Mississippi Delta (and they, contrary to the common labels, are not bad kids either).

Americans are plain bad at interacting across socioeconomic and racial lines. If a Harvard grad from Connecticut is able to leap over that inevitable hurdle, then he is a certain kind of hero. But if he—understandably—can't, he's a disservice to everyone.

The TFA line on this is that even corps members who choose not to continue teaching or don't feel particularly effective will have hard-earned respect for how difficult teaching is. "It has the potential to open people's eyes to a different reality," Dena admits. But she points out another danger: "This guy from Wisconsin or wherever does Teach for America and then goes home, and his family is like, 'Oh my God, you teach those brown kids in the Bronx! What is that like?' It perpetuates the stereotypes that they came in with rather than dispelling them."

Another of Dena's pet peeves is when TFA teachers refer to their students as "these kids."

She questions them: "Don't you mean *our* kids?"

DENA'S KIDS GO ON A TOUR of the Middlebury campus, led by a blonde, blue-eyed jock named Chris. By the end, some of them are trailing far behind; but a small group of swooning girls stays right up front, following Chris's every move. When he tells them that he plays Quidditch, like the characters in the Harry Potter series—complete with brooms and capes—the girls look at one another with alarm and start speaking in rapid Spanish so Chris won't know what they're saying (*What is he talking about? I don't know, but he's cute.*). Even his dorm room, which has that distinct college smell of B.O. and microwave popcorn, doesn't turn them off. When he ends the tour, he asks, "Any other questions?"

Deasia responds, "Can we take a picture of you?"

He blushes and moves as if to pose with them, but they say, "No, just you." He stands alone and awkward against the tableau of a busy cafeteria—a college student prototype captured in his native environment.

After the students consume piles of pizza and fried chicken, ice cream and cupcakes (everywhere we go on campus, they devour mountains of free food), we head to a college course titled "Writing and Social Change," taught by one of Dena's favorite former professors, Catharine Wright. Before the students walk into the room, Dena pauses at the head of the line, her hand on the doorknob, and says to them, "Where are we from?" Before they can answer, she goes on: "The Bronx. And we're amazing, and we're going to show them what we're made of." They all enter, heads held high.

When it's time for introductions, John mumbles, "I like to make inventions."

Hema says, "To make a long story short, I love to be creative," with characteristic flair.

Professor Wright goes on and on about what an incredible person Dena is: "extremely extraordinary." She says, "She's won every award and prestigious fellowship there is. She's going on to graduate school . . ." She trails off when she sees Dena's alarmed face. "Or maybe not. Maybe someday she'll go on to graduate school. The rumor around Middlebury is that she will be the United States Secretary of Education." The students seem suspicious, but are too thrown off by the last grand declaration about their teacher to follow up.

ONE DAY, AS DENA AND I sit and discuss her time working in overcrowded maternity wards in Santo Domingo and interviewing sex workers in Antigua and battling the forces of abuse and addiction that her students bring in like home-packed lunches day in and day out, I halt the flow of conversation and ask Dena, "Are you afraid of anything?"

She looks at me quizzically and asks back, "Do you think I'm *not* afraid of *anything*?"

I shake my head no, and she lets out a huge laugh. After

thinking for a moment, she says, "If I'm walking alone at night in dark places, I'm scared to get attacked. Typical city fears. I don't like to be in an elevator with a strange man. That would be scary."

"But do you have any emotional fears? Fear of failure, for example?"

She shakes her head defiantly. "I think failure is an opportunity to learn. Nothing came easy for me growing up. Getting where I am wasn't easy. People always talked down to me, assumed I was younger than I was or less intelligent. I always had to do double work. So I have this fighter attitude."

Dena often invokes the spirit of her family—women fighting against the odds. I'm astounded at the amount of energy she has, how fearless she is, the extent to which she throws herself into teaching and doesn't let her limitations (not being able to control what goes on outside the classroom) frustrate her. Her mother's legacy—being ridiculed, raped, abandoned—and her twin sister's suffering—both the illness and the ill treatment by medical professionals—seem to have rooted themselves deep in her psyche, pushing her every day to prove that everyone, especially the often maligned and forgotten children of the Bronx, is of immeasurable value. She can't change what has happened to the women she loves most, but she can make sure that no one else feels that way as long as she's around.

But how long will she be around?

She's still puzzling over the decision about grad school for the following fall. Though she's put in her deposit at Teacher's College, just so she can hold her spot, she's still not sure whether she's going to go through with it. In an e-mail in mid-May, she writes, "It's sooooo hard to leave the classroom, to not be here in the South Bronx where there are so many children in need of someone to care for them. I still haven't made a final decision."

AFTER THE KIDS HAVE DINNER with their homestay families—a motley collection of professors, staff people, and a few townies—they all rendezvous again at the Kenyon Arena, a 2,600-seat ice skating rink on campus. Kenyon has been converted into a massive hootenanny—the ice covered over, haystacks and camping tents brought in—for the American Cancer Society's annual Relay for Life. (This year's theme is the Wild West.) Members of teams—book club gals with matching white Keds, Middlebury swimmers with giant shoulder muscles, teenagers with thick black eyeliner, all smelling of adolescent ulterior motives—will take turns walking in incessant circles around the arena from 6:00 p.m. until 9:00 a.m. In the center of the arena is a stage where college bands, DJs, dance teams, and other local spectacles will keep everyone entertained. Dena has arranged for about half a dozen of her girls to perform the dance number that they recently unveiled at a student showcase.

But first there's the jam band to get through. A tall guy with shaggy blonde hair and a Seattle Seahawks jersey is doing a rock-style cover of OutKast's "Hey Ya!" Dena thinks it's hilarious; she's dancing like a fool, flailing her elbows and jumping around. One of the girls leans over to me and says, "Sometimes she's like a big sister, because she's so cool. But then sometimes she's like a mom, because she's so embarrassing."

John tries to get her attention as she dips and swirls. "Miss Simmons, can we go back to the Bronx now?"

When about half of the girls take the stage, the other half sit near me in plastic folding chairs and fret about what is about to happen. "I hope they're not too sexy," Hema says.

"I know—when they performed for the school, all the boys were staring at their breasts," her sister Deepa agrees, looking around apprehensively. Indeed, a huge crowd of people has gathered around—middle-aged, white, expectant.

I flash back to 2006, when journalist Lawrence Downes wrote

a *New York Times* piece about being scandalized while watching a talent show at his daughter's middle school in which girls "writhe and strut, shake their bottoms, splay their legs, thrust their chests out and in and out again." It was the most e-mailed article for weeks. I send a little prayer up to nowhere: "Please don't let the people standing around here have that reaction." The visit has been pretty magical up till now. I don't want to see it melt into cultural confusion.

Dena sits on the floor in front of the chairs like a stage mother, smiling up at the six dancers, all dressed in pink tank tops or T-shirts. She helped them choreograph the dance after school over a period of months—yet another unpaid investment in the kids. She doesn't seem worried at all.

The dance—set to Missy Elliot's "Lose Control"—goes off without a hitch. It's a little sexy, but the girls who were fretting are relieved; the dancers must have intuitively toned everything down a notch, recognizing that their audience might not be ready for full-blown Bronx-style popping. The crowd goes wild for the out-of-town guests. Dena stands and claps as if she's just witnessed three acts of Alvin Ailey. Everyone runs off to get more free food—burgers and hot dogs and fudge brownies.

DENA ISN'T COMING BACK to teach next year. She and Mr. Kelly, the principal, had a series of meetings, trying to figure out a way to keep her on staff at the Urban Science Academy while she also pursued her EdD at Teachers College, but it simply can't be done. Budget cuts have made everything very tight, and even a part-time position would be too much of a stretch.

She finally admitted it to me in mid-July, after every possible alternative had been exhausted. She wrote in an e-mail, "This has been one of the hardest decisions I have ever had to make." In the end, she decided that even if there had been a way to keep teaching, it wouldn't have been a good idea. "I would have probably ignored my own studies," Dena said, pointing out that the sum of her student loans is so huge that she wants to make sure she makes the most of her time at Columbia and gets through the program as quickly as possible. Mr. Kelly has promised that he will always hire her back if she wants to return.

She went on, "It's important work and someone needs to do it, but for me to believe that I'm the best and brightest and that the whole world is going to collapse if I leave is very egotistical. There are a whole batch of capable individuals who will come after me."

And of course, Dena can never stay away from teaching entirely. She'd already set up a tutoring position in a public school in Harlem for two hours a day. "I will still be working with children, teaching them and learning from them," she assured me. And herself.

TO FOCUS ON THE INTERSECTION of health and education seems infinitely valuable. While Dena's classroom is a truly unusual haven of respect, learning, and joy, the world outside of it continues to put her students through hell. You can see subtle signs of the lives they lead outside Classroom 823 if you watch and listen closely enough—the other teachers who don't bother answering their questions, the narrative essays filled with the absence of fathers, the vacillation between not being grown up enough (more than a couple of them still suck their thumbs at thirteen years old) and growing up too fast (worrying over the ramifications of being too sexy), the plates piled high with fried and greasy foods, the posture of depression—a kid curled in on himself, unengaged, checked out. Dena has tried, for example, for three years to get Chris's parents to acknowledge that he is suffering from clinical depression and get him the help he needs, but to no avail.

When I spoke to Principal Kelly, he admitted, "The level of

untreated illness in this community is devastating. The level of support that a school can offer is woefully inadequate."

Dena echoes, "I've always been about education, education, education, but there needs to be a marriage between health and education. I'd love to create a health and education cooperative in the Bronx someday."

"Do you think you'll ever leave the Bronx?" I ask.

"I don't know," Dena says, smiling. "There's something special about being from the Bronx and continuing to live here even when you don't have to. It's about choosing to live there. I *choose* to live in the Bronx."

Dena has been feeling deeply conflicted about her decision to leave teaching. She's a teacher. It's in her blood. "I feel like I'm giving up a part of myself by not teaching next year," she says, "and I feel like I'm letting down all of the seventh graders who dreamed of having me as a teacher.

"Also, I'm leaving a stable job and giving up my tenure in a very tough economy. But I have to find hope in the fact that I will be pursuing more education so that I could be a more effective, efficient, and available giver to the world."

AS THE BUS PULLS AWAY from Middlebury and down the winding road past the admissions office, past the cafeteria, past the arena and the golf course, the kids settle into their seats—appendages thrown over one another, exhausted and grass-stained from the final rolls and races down the sloping hills of impeccable grass. Dena had a cutthroat race with the four tallest boys in the class, their long legs carrying them far ahead of her. "We racing!" Darien screamed over his shoulder as Dena struggled to catch up.

She yelled ahead at him, "You forgot a verb!"

"We're racing!" Darien corrected himself, still in flight.

Now in the bus, they look spent, like they have experienced lifetimes in the last twenty-four hours. I look back and wonder how much of it will stick with them, how much of it will impact their academic performance in high school, their ability to take the road less traveled out of the Bronx, even if it leads them back again, as it did Dena. Just one day at Middlebury can't change a kid's life, can it?

Then again, three years with a truly exceptional teacher can. It has to. One of them shouts, "Thank you, Miss Simmons!" and prompts a chorus of gratitude and love from the others: "Yeah, thank you, Miss Simmons! Bye, Middlebury! Bye, cute white boys! Bye, grass! We love you, Miss Simmons!"

Conclusion
Good Failure

My parents and I were lingering at the breakfast table, a haphazard arrangement of toast crumbs, empty coffee cups, and crumpled sections of the newspaper littered about, having our ten millionth conversation about activism. Silver-haired and laugh-lined now, my parents had once protested the Vietnam War, agitated for an admissions policy that would diversify their college campus, and staged a sit-in to get beer at the student center. I asked them, "Okay, I want you to be real with me. You *actually* believed that you could change the world?"

My dad looked me right in the eyes and said, nodding his head emphatically, "Courtney, we actually believed we *were* changing the world."

It was as foreign to me as Mars. The surety of that time, the faith in conviction, action, and outcome were impossible, as far as I was concerned, in today's messy world. Contemporary efforts at social change often seem like going into a black hole. It's easy to get lost once you're sucked in—consider all the complexities, the danger of good intentions, the comprehensive impact of multinational corporations, the ethical quagmires around every corner (*What do I eat? What do I wear? Where do I live? Whom do I befriend?*). It's easy to surrender to the darkness, exhausted by all the self-examination and economic and political analysis. It's easy to feel like failure is inevitable.

And here's the surprising thing: working on this book for the past couple of years—spending time with these incredible people, hearing about the defining moments of their lives, asking them probing questions, reveling in their earnest answers—has only confirmed my suspicion that failure is, indeed, usually inevitable. What's changed is my understanding of the nature of failure.

For Raul, Richard's death was a failure of sorts, but it gave him a depth of feeling that allows him to sit in the most alienating of settings and connect with the most hardened of young men. Emily was a failure at social work—it left her embittered and uninspired; she needed that experience in order to move toward her real calling in filmmaking. Nia failed to get the climate change bill she really wanted. Tyrone failed to give away all of his money.

"Yes, it's failure, but how good a failure?" philosopher Cornel West asks filmmaker Astra Taylor in her documentary *Examined Life*. It turns out that there is no surefire way to "do good" in the twenty-first century. There are no pat or pure answers. There are no true heroes—and those who cast themselves in this light probably haven't thought hard enough about the complexities of their work or explored the terrain of their own souls with enough honesty. There are only occasional triumphs and, more often, good failures.

Good failures are what you achieve when you aim to transform an entire broken system and end up healing one broken soul. They are the small victories—Arturo strapping on his fire boots and setting off for another day of wilderness training, an utterly foreign feeling of accomplishment washing over him; a college kid who has always pretended that she struggled with money finally being honest with her best friend about her trust fund and having an electrifying conversation about her plans to become part of the social justice philanthropy movement; a young woman insisting that her boyfriend put on a condom after seeing Emily Abt's film about HIV/AIDS rates; one of Dena's former students sitting in the office with his guidance counselor on the first day of high school and saying, "I plan on going to college. Can you help me plan a schedule that will get me there?"

It's not that we shouldn't aim to transform the prison-industrial complex, reduce wealth disparity in this country, cure HIV and AIDS, fix public education. It's that we must hold these large-scale revolutions in our hearts while tackling small, radical acts every day with our hands. We must wake up wondering how we might fail at changing absolutely everything in such a way that we manage to change a little something.

ACKNOWLEDGE SUFFERING

There is so much pain in this unfinished world full of systemic racism, sexism, and classism, of fearful, desperate men and women. Maricela's rape is a shattering example of how toxic our culture can be for people, how it can push us to violate one another with such severity and long-lasting consequences. The fact that Dena's kids have to live in a neighborhood where there is never enough money, never enough food, never enough safety is a testament to our collective failure as a nation. Dena bravely battles these conditions every day, but the fact is that these conditions should not exist. Period. Raul should never have to listen to another young man describe being molested as a child.

Suffering, as Buddhists believe, is an intrinsic and undeniable part of our human experience. It does no one any good to deny this reality, nor does it do anyone any good to romanticize it. Guilt doesn't put food on anyone's table. Self-negation or playing small doesn't actually make room for others—it makes the room less authentic. Instead, we must all face the truth of suffering head-on, eyes wide, hearts open.

Our first, and perhaps most difficult, task as modern-day activists is to truly sit with the pain of the world. We spend so

much of our lives inside our own pain—experiencing it, drama-
tizing it, numbing it, talking about it, trying desperately to heal
it. Activism is, in part, an exercise in putting a fraction of that
same energy into the honoring of pain outside of ourselves. It is
about listening deeply, investing time in really understanding another person's experience of the world, not turning away from the
inconvenient truths of contemporary suffering or turning them
into reality television narratives (see *Extreme Makeover: Home
Edition,* where every pain is disappeared with a monstrous living
room set).

Of course, ultimately, the suffering in others that we are most
affected by is somehow related to our own—consciously or not.
As James Baldwin wrote, "One can only face in others what one
can face in oneself. On this confrontation depends the measure
of our wisdom and compassion. This energy is all that one finds in
the rubble of vanished civilizations, and the only hope for ours."

HUMANIZE PEOPLE

Each human being is a world. Part of truly creating a more just
world is recognizing this and cultivating our capacity to honor it
in everyone we meet—despite all the forces that push us to move
faster, pay less attention, get less involved. Hearing all of these
individuals' stories, and watching them hear the stories of others,
was the most powerful part of the experience. I think we all made
the world better just by sitting and listening, by being fully present and open to being amazed by people's capacity to overcome
pain, confront cruelty with ingenuity and kindness, become
more honest, more accountable, more wise.

"I do battle," wrote Frantz Fanon, "for creation of a human
world—that is, a world of reciprocal recognition." Each of these
eight people has joined Fanon in that epic and moral struggle
to truly see others and, in turn, to be truly seen. These eight

practitioners have different ways of evaluating their own successes. Ever pragmatic, there have been times when I've twisted myself into knots trying to understand how I might evaluate their effectiveness. Does Nia's disappointment in the weak standards contained in the Waxman-Markey bill mean her work was for naught? If Dena's students don't make it to college, will she have failed? If Raul's clients get sucked back into the gang life, will his commitment be wasted? There's a tendency in this culture to see success only on a grand scale. I like what Michelle Kuo wrote about this in *Letters from Young Activists:*

> I worry whether my own vision is vast enough. But then I pause, and think: smallness is underrated. So much—too much—is given undue largeness. Even that phrase of ours, "public service," has too much heft to it. For whom do we claim to serve? At times, I am startled by how scarcely I know the people I "serve," how boldly I abstract and sociologize. I must live for that glimpse of how vast a single person is.

Each of the people these activists "serve" is, indeed, vast—as are they. Ultimately, I'd rather humanize Nia and Dena and Raul than nitpick their methods. There are enough people, to return to the wisdom of Jane Addams, who "smother the divine fire of youth." I've found that the empathy I've developed for each of these activists, as I've learned their stories and vicariously experienced their struggles, has given me more empathy for myself in this journey toward social justice. It's made me less strident, less righteous, less hard on myself.

I can still see the road of overthinking, despair, paralysis, just off to the right, but I manage to avoid it most days. I manage instead to take the road of dogged pursuit of impossible dreams. There's a whole generation of us here, putting one foot in front of the other and doing our damned best to live meaningful lives in honor of our own gifts and in pursuit of justice.

UNDERSTAND BACKWARD, BUT LIVE FORWARD

The legacy that these activists carry with them, to one extent or another, is the 1960s-era activism that has become so iconic, and in some ways distorted, in its constant retelling. Vietnam War protests, civil rights marches, black power, and feminist struggles have been resurrected in word, image, and emotion for decades now—creating a sort of superactivist standard to which the activists of later generations inevitably compare themselves. This theme shows up most lucidly for Tyrone and Nia; they strain to define themselves in relationship to, but also separate from, a legacy of radical foremothers and forefathers. On one hand, they find inspiration; on the other, they find dangerous sentimentalizing.

Dan Berger writes, "A mythology of the Sixties is unhelpful, even detrimental, to any attempts at understanding what happened, let alone to forging progressive movement strategy today." We simply live in a different world. With different weather—a perfect storm of cultural, economic, environmental, and psychosocial fronts that combine to create the context for all of our action. We can attempt to integrate what was learned, but we must resist replication. We must resist the urge to contrast our activist experiences directly with theirs; it's like expecting an iPod to be a record player. There are things lost—the raw scratching and visceral touch—and things gained—breadth and depth, options, portability.

Besides, the sixties were never as effective or simple as the mythologized stories make them sound. History has a way of smoothing itself out, hyping itself up, being set to an emotionally manipulative soundtrack. Must we live forever in the shadow of that cinematic version of radical activism? No. Is it under-standable that we might be jealous of the collective and visceral experiences of that time, the conviction that kids really did have power to challenge authority and change the world? Of course. And they did. In some ways they succeeded so profoundly that it's hard to imagine America before—a time when only married women were allowed to get birth control and we'd never had an African American senator, much less an African American president. This is why many of us watch the AMC hit show *Mad Men* with such utter bewilderment; my jaw literally dropped when I saw Don and Betty Draper throw their picnic trash on the grass before heading home. The world has been transformed for the better.

But the activists of the sixties and seventies also had their good failures. They didn't succeed in truly integrating public schools, but they did win *Brown v. Board of Education*. They didn't get the Equal Rights Amendment passed, but they did shift cultural expectations of women—professionally, domesti-cally, sexually. They didn't move "back to the land" for long; so many of those idealistic young hippies ended up ditching the backhoes for 401(k)s and vacation homes when it was all said and done. The wonderful consolation is that a critical mass of good failures adds up to grand successes—systemic change like that ushered in during the sixties, which has created an entirely different world for us to grow up in than the one our parents struggled through.

We can hope for that same kind of transformative accumula-tion for our own children. After all, we are writing our own narra-tives right here. They may be less dramatic, less sun-dappled or orgiastic than the ones our parents wrote, but they are inspired, and they are ours. In fact, there's something really special about owning an activist identity in this time and place. Unlike the ac-tivists of the past, the young people featured here are not swept up in a movement inevitable as the tide. They have had to define their values and figure out how to live them in a proactive way. They haven't stumbled into the protest marches alongside their best friends and drinking buddies; they have sought out opportunities to affect legislation, educate the public, rebuild, teach—often on their own, often in contradiction to the youth culture they are surrounded by.

DREAM UNREASONABLY, BUT PROCEED STRATEGICALLY

Everyone seems to be struggling, in one way or another, with questions of scale. Raised in the bigger, faster eighties, it's not surprising that we are attracted to big bangs. Tyrone wants to destabilize capitalism. Rachel wanted to create peace in the Middle East. Nia wants to save the planet. Rosario wants to stop rape in the Congo. You've got to admire our generational gumption.

The danger in our big dreams, of course, is the inevitable disappointment. Resilience, above all else, is the lifeblood of the contemporary activist. Strategic realism often gets a bad rap in do-gooder circles, but I think it's a necessary tool of the young person craving change in America today. Maricela, for example, will continue to try to change military culture, but meanwhile she will work with others to create an organization that serves those broken by it. Nia will continue to preach about eco-apartheid, but also make relationships with mostly white environmental groups if it means that the work progresses. Rosario will use her celebrity and beauty in a world that still puts a ridiculously high premium on both, all while subverting people's expectations of her.

There is an enlightened duality in so many of these activists' approaches—a duality that allows them to retain their native sense of idealism while still fighting in a way that doesn't lead them to despair. Their big dreams are secured to the real world by a thousand daily anchors of small acts.

Another question that surfaces repeatedly in these stories of goodwill and hard work is about community: where can we contribute the most and with whom?

We can use our own ingenuity to find communities in which we feel a sense of interdependence, coupled with some bright ideas about ways to improve the quality of life for everyone. This doesn't mean that you can't do work outside of your own little slice of identity, but it does mean that you seriously consider—as have so many of the activists in this book—the ways in which some of the most difficult and powerful activism starts within your own family, your own neighborhood, your own class demographic.

No one can do Raul's job like he does—soothing the fears of young men who come from his own neighborhood. And similarly, no one can do Tyrone's job like he has—getting young people with wealth to rigorously examine their own values. Dena is such a successful educator because, in part, she knows the smells, sounds, and tastes of her students' lives intimately.

This approach also requires humbly recognizing when your background, set of experiences, or educational achievements don't actually prepare you to do the best work in a given community. Sometimes our most profound actions on the road to justice are actually inaction, our most profound words those that were never spoken so that others could have the space to speak. It's important to have an accurate picture of who you have the capacity to reach, rather than expending a bunch of precious energy on trying to reach absolutely everyone.

Activists are not interchangeable. It's time that our generation embraced our respective limitations, not as signs of weakness but as valuable information as we pursue lives of meaning. We must resist exoticizing the suffering outside of our own circles or overestimating our own specialness. Just because we are Americans, just because we come from some modicum of privilege (almost anyone living in the United States has some privilege to come to terms with), doesn't mean we are equipped to solve all of the world's problems.

We must learn to listen to ourselves. The moments when these eight people felt most effective were inevitably the moments when they gave up trying to enact someone else's revolution. Emily was meant to be behind a camera, not a desk, and until she accepted that, she was miserable. When Nia stands in front of a room and talks about why people of color are disproportionately affected by climate change, you can actually hear her words being lifted up by an innate passion—something that could never be taught in a public speaking course. And when I stopped wallowing in my own sense of helplessness and started researching, interviewing people, writing it all down, I reawakened to my own calling.

This is what Frederick Buechner means when he talks about that intersection where "your deep gladness and the world's deep hunger meet." The world needs art, inspiration, stories. It needs frank conversations about race, it needs clean water and air, it needs analysis of social justice work in contemporary America. And we three—Emily, Nia, and I—are glad in that provision. We thrive in our sense of being needed by this country that we love and expect so much more from. The good news is that our gifts and the world's needs are so diverse that we can pursue our own intersections while trusting that others will flourish where we would have floundered.

Beyond our individual stories, our unique gladness and gifts, there is an insatiable hunger for community among our generation. There are skeptics who believe that technological advances and rapid globalization have actually served to distance us from one another, to make us less community oriented and more digitally isolated. Our generation is especially targeted in this narrative; we're too busy text messaging, blogging about our sex lives, and wreaking havoc in video games—or so the hyperbolic news stories go—to actually look up and engage with one another.

But getting to know these eight people, watching them move through their respective worlds, I couldn't disagree more. Even those who use technology do so to connect with others and create real-time, face-to-face transformation. Raul, Maricela, Rosario, Dena—all of them are deeply, profoundly imbedded in the communities that they've chosen and cultivated. In so many respects, their communities *are* their activism. Communities heal these activists, inspire them, outrage them, challenge them, and honor them. They allow them to sustain such difficult work through the engine of common purpose and "reciprocal recognition" (just as Fanon envisioned it).

Doing social justice work is a huge psychological risk. I was repeatedly shattered, throughout the research and writing of this book, at how much emotional pain all of these people have had to endure in order to do their work, make their art, speak their truths. There are so many stories of heartbreak, burnout, defeat, and resurrection that echo one another cross-issue, cross-place, cross-spirit. This is one more reason that being imbedded in communities is so critical for these young visionaries. They must have people to go to when the obstacles seem too huge, the opposition too powerful, the world too unconscious or uncaring. Without one another, we risk bitterness. With one another, we have the opportunity to stay vulnerable, stay determined, stay the course.

CULTIVATE IMPATIENCE AND ENDURANCE

The strangest thing happened on the way to my thirties. I real-ized that I wasn't going to live forever. And it made the prospect of paralysis—the option of overthinking and wallowing in my own disillusion about what I'd been told, in contrast to what I was observing and experiencing—all seem like a whole lot of wasted time. Certainly there is need for reflection, research, and self-examination before we jump too enthusiastically into "do-ing good," but we are also a generation with a tendency to stew. We've learned how to analyze well, perhaps too well, thanks to our curricula in critical thinking and our hard-working teachers. We can intellectualize any solution into tatters with our finely sharpened swords of cultural relativity. And it's honorable that we've got these skills and that we're not afraid to use them.

But as George Jackson says, "Patience has its limits. Take it too far, and it's cowardice." We must be fearless in both our analysis and our action. We must accept that we will fail and try anyway, try to fail always more exquisitely, more honestly, more effectively. We must wake up in the morning naively believing in the power of our own dreams and the potential of our own gifts, and go to bed exhausted and determined to do it all over again—with maybe just a bit of a different tactic, a little less ego, a little more help.

What else are you going to do? Give up?

Of course you're not. You're not going to do that, because you are part of a long line of people who didn't do that, because you live in a country that was actually founded on the assumption that you would be audacious and rebellious and inexhaustible in your pursuit of a more perfect union. You're not going to settle, because you've seen how that kills people, how resigning and consuming and forgetting are surefire ways to deaden a soul. You're not going to give up, because it would be terribly boring. You're not going to give up, because you owe the world, this nation, yourself, bravery in the face of suffering, vision in the face of stagnancy, and blood, sweat, and tears in the face of injustice. The good failure is your debt for being here. Now. In this beautiful, horrible place.

We each have the opportunity to live our lives consciously in spite of all the soporific influences, to act even when we know how complex the prospect of doing so truly is. Our charge is not to "save the world," after all; it is to live in it, flawed and fierce, loving and humble. As children of the eighties and nineties, we are uniquely positioned to fail. The bureaucracy we face, the scale of our challenges, the intractable nature of so many of our most unjust international institutions and systems—all these add up to colossal potential for disappointment. No matter. We must strive to make the world better anyway. We must struggle to make our friendships, our families, our neighborhoods, our cities, and our nation more dignified, knowing that it might not work and struggling anyway. We must dedicate ourselves each and every morning to being the most kind, thoughtful, courageous human beings who have ever walked the earth, and know that it still won't be enough. We must do it anyway.

Acknowledgments

As Dena's student so wisely put it, "Everyone says love is a big word. One way it works is to make everything better than before." I am surrounded by big-hearted, sharp-minded people who make everything better than before on a daily basis. It is my absolute pleasure to thank them whenever I get the chance.

Tracy Brown, my literary agent, had enough of his own youthful adventures as a taxi driver, farmhand, and activist to appreciate my need to do this book. I so appreciate his patience as I searched for the right way to tell the stories of my generation. And it is Amy Caldwell of Beacon Press who deserves all the credit for zeroing in on the right way. She's an engaged, thoughtful editor and friend. Thanks to all those at the truly unique Beacon Press who have done such a tremendous job in shaping this book and spreading the word.

Thanks to Pamela Tanner Boll, who is not only a mentor but a true partner in the world. You continually astound me with your artistry, generosity, and vision. And thanks to all of my mentors: Robin Stern, Janet Patti, Selena Sermeno, Deborah Siegel, Gloria Feldt, Kristal Brent Zook, and so many others. Thanks to the whole gang at the Women's Media Center for your support and wisdom. Thank you to all the SSCP secret agents, especially 1979 and Co., for all the generous scheming.

I raise a huge glass of wine and a giant slice of pizza in toasting my writer's group, who edited almost every one of these profiles with great care and shrewd criticism. Our crew is such a fine example of the surprising power of people gathering in a room and taking one another seriously (and not so seriously, when that's what's in order). Thank you to every one of you for the commitment you've made to your own work and each other.

Special thanks to Ramin Hedayati for being eternally wide-eyed, Megan Hinton for twenty years and counting, and the Feministing crew—Jessica, Vanessa, Samhita, Perez, Ann, and the next generation—for having my back and making me better. Friedman, you can edit me anytime, anyplace. Thanks to all of my incredible friends—Gareth, Kate, Christina, the crew—who have protested, discussed, and danced our twenties away. As it should be.

Thanks to Nikolai Johnson for coproducing my greatest failure so far. You provided a home for me during all these years of wandering.

Thanks to Chris Roan, my favorite guy to share a burger and a brainstorm with. You make everything seem possible. Thanks to Daniel May, who has shaped my ideas about activism, altruism, and ethics in such profound ways. You help me answer what I thought were my deepest questions and then ask much harder ones. Thanks to Mary X for being the angel next door.

Thanks to the Bellagio Center of the Rockefeller Foundation and all the incredible people I met there. One in particular: Mr. Cary, your editing, adoration, and faith are truly dangerous. You are the absolute embodiment of doing it anyway. See you at the Belvedere.

Thanks to my brother for every time I didn't light myself on fire, my momma for teaching me about community, and my papa for never losing the outraged twenty-year-old within. Without you all, I'd be ranting on a hillside in New Mexico somewhere alone. As it is, I never am.

ACKNOWLEDGMENTS

Finally, thanks to the people who opened their lives and their hearts to me during the course of writing this book. Your trust means the world.

Further Resources

ORGANIZATIONS

Casa Atabex Aché
casaatabexache.org

Enough
www.enoughenough.org

Environmental Justice and Climate Change Initiative
www.ejcc.org

Homeboy Industries
www.homeboy-industries.org

Lower Eastside Girls Club
www.girlsclub.org

Pureland Pictures
www.purelandpictures.com

Resource Generation
www.resourcegeneration.org

Service Women's Action Network (SWAN)
www.servicewomen.org

V-Day
www.vday.org

Voto Latino
www.votolatino.org

FURTHER READING AND WATCHING

Books

Addams, Jane. *The Spirit of Youth and the City Streets*. Champaign, IL: University of Illinois Press, 2001. Orig. published 1921.

Baldwin, James. *Nobody Knows My Name*. New York: Dell, 1962.

Benedict, Helen. *The Lonely Soldier: The Private War of Women Serving in Iraq*. Boston: Beacon Press, 2009.

Benjamin, Medea, and Jodie Evans, eds. *Stop the Next War Now: Effective Responses to Violence and Terrorism*. Makawao, Maui, HI: Inner Ocean Publishing, 2005.

Berger, Dan. *Outlaws of America: The Weather Underground and the Politics of Solidarity*. Oakland, CA: AK Press, 2006.

Berger, Dan, Chesa Boudin, and Kenyon Farrow, eds. *Letters from Young Activists: Today's Rebels Speak Out*. New York: Nation Books, 2005.

Bornstein, David. *How to Change the World: Social Entrepreneurs and the Power of New Ideas*. Updated ed. New York: Oxford University Press, 2007.

Boyle, Gregory. *Tattoos on the Heart: The Power of Boundless Compassion*. New York: Free Press, 2010.

Browne, Jaron, Marisa Franco, Jason Negrón-Gonzales, and Steve Williams. *Towards Land, Work, and Power: Charting a Path of Resistance to U.S.-Led Imperialism*. San Francisco: Unite to Fight Press, 2005.

Buechner, Frederick. *Wishful Thinking: A Seeker's ABC.* New York: HarperOne, 1993.

Coetzee, J. M. *Waiting for the Barbarians.* New York: Penguin, 1982.

Connery, Michael. *Youth to Power: How Today's Young Voters Are Building Tomorrow's Progressive Majority.* Brooklyn, NY: Ig Publishing, 2008.

Corrie, Rachel. *Let Me Stand Alone: The Journals of Rachel Corrie.* New York: W. W. Norton, 2009.

Ensler, Eve, ed. *A Memory, a Monologue, a Rant, and a Prayer.* New York: Villard Books, 2007.

Fanon, Frantz. *Black Skin, White Masks.* New York: Grove Press, 2008. Orig. published 1952.

Fremon, Celeste. *G-Dog and the Homeboys: Father Greg Boyle and the Gangs of East Los Angeles.* Rev. ed. Albuquerque: University of New Mexico Press, 2008.

Gray-Garcia, Lisa ("Tiny"). *Criminal of Poverty: Growing Up Homeless in America.* San Francisco: City Lights Foundation Books, 2006.

INCITE! Women of Color Against Violence, ed. *The Revolution Will Not Be Funded: Beyond the Non-Profit Industrial Complex.* Cambridge, MA: South End Press, 2007.

———. *Color of Violence: The INCITE! Anthology.* Cambridge, MA: South End Press, 2006.

Jackson, George. *Soledad Brother: The Prison Letters of George Jackson.* New York: Bantam, 1972.

Kelley, Robin D. G. *Freedom Dreams: The Black Radical Imagination*. Boston: Beacon Press, 2002.

Kim, Jee, Mathilda de Dios, Pablo Caraballo, Manuela Arciniegas, Ibrahim Abdul-Matin, and Kofi Taha. *Future 500: Youth Organizing and Activism in the United States*. New Orleans: New Mouth from the Dirty South/Garrett County Press, 2002.

Klein, Naomi. *The Shock Doctrine: The Rise of Disaster Capitalism*. New York: Metropolitan Books, 2007.

Lui, Meizhu, Bárbara Robies, Betsy Leondar-Wright, Rose Brewer, and Rebecca Adamson, with United for a Fair Economy. *The Color of Wealth: The Story Behind the U.S. Racial Wealth Divide*. New York: New Press, 2006.

McIntyre, Alasdair. *After Virtue*. Notre Dame, IN: University of Notre Dame Press, 1984. 2nd edition.

Morgan, Edward P. *The 60s Experience: Hard Lessons about Modern America*. Philadelphia: Temple University Press, 1991.

Nichtern, Ethan. *One City: A Declaration of Interdependence*. Somerville, MA: Wisdom Publications, 2007.

Palmer, Parker J. *Let Your Life Speak: Listening for the Voice of Vocation*. San Francisco: Jossey-Bass, 1999.

Pittelman, Karen, and Resource Generation. *Classified: How to Stop Hiding Your Privilege and Use It for Social Change!* New York: Soft Skull Press, 2006.

Putnam, Robert D. *Bowling Alone: The Collapse and Revival of American Community*. New York: Simon & Schuster, 2000.

Solnit, Rebecca. *Hope in the Dark: Untold Histories, Wild Possibilities*. New York: Nation Books, 2004.

Films

All of Us. DVD. Directed by Emily Abt. New York: Pureland Pictures, 2007.

Explicit Ills. DVD. Directed by Mark Webber; starring Rosario Dawson. Los Angeles: Peace Arch Home Entertainment, 2009.

Take It from Me. DVD. Directed by Emily Abt. New York: Pureland Pictures, 2001.

Toe to Toe. Directed by Emily Abt. Los Angeles: Strand Releasing, 2009.

V-Day: Until the Violence Stops. DVD. Directed by Abby Epstein. New York: New Video, 2005.

The Weather Underground. DVD. Directed by Sam Green and Bill Siegel. New York: New Video, 2004.